USING LATEX TO WRITE A PhD THESIS

NICOLA L. C. TALBOT

VOLUME 2 OF
THE DICKIMAW LATEX SERIES

DICKIMAW BOOKS

SAXLINGHAM NETHERGATE

British Library Cataloguing in Publication Data
Talbot, Nicola L. C., b. 1970
Using LaTeX to Write a PhD Thesis
Volume 2 of The Dickimaw LaTeX Series

ISBN 978-1-909440-02-9
BIC: UGD — Desktop publishing
1. LaTeX (Computer file); 2. Computerized typesetting.

Published by Dickimaw Books.

CONTENTS

LIST OF FIGURES

LIST OF TABLES

LISTINGS

ABSTRACT

This book is aimed at PhD students who want to use LaTeX to typeset their PhD thesis. If you are unfamiliar with LaTeX I recommend that you first read Volume 1: *LaTeX for Complete Novices* [15].

CHAPTER 1

INTRODUCTION

Many PhD students in the sciences are encouraged to produce their PhD thesis in LaTeX, particularly if their work involves a lot of mathematics. In addition, these days, LaTeX is no longer the sole province of mathematicians and computer scientists and is now starting to be used in the arts and social sciences (see, for example, some of the topics listed in the TeX online catalogue [3]). This book is intended as a brief guide on how to typeset the various components that are usually required for a thesis. If you have never used LaTeX before, I recommend that you first read Volume 1: *LaTeX for Complete Novices* [15], as this book assumes you have a basic knowledge of LaTeX. As with Volume 1, I'll be using PDFLaTeX and TeXWorks. If you are creating a DVI file or you are using a different editor, you'll have to adapt the instructions.

If you are unfamiliar with terms such as "preamble", read Volume 1 [15, §2]. If you don't know how to find package documentation, read Volume 1 [15, §1.1].

Throughout this document there are pointers to related topics in the UK List of TeX Frequently Asked Questions[1.1] (UK FAQ). These are displayed in the margin in square brackets, as illustrated on the right. You may find these resources useful in answering related questions that are not covered in this book. To find the resources, go to http://www.tex.ac.uk/faq and either look for the question title in the list, or enter a keyword in the search field.

[FAQ: What is LaTeX?]

On-line versions of this book, along with associated files, are available at: http://www.dickimaw-books.com/latex/thesis/.

To refresh your memory or for those who haven't read Volume 1, throughout this book source code is illustrated in a typewriter font with the word Input placed in the margin, and the corresponding output (how it will appear in the PDF document) is typeset with the word Output in the margin.

EXAMPLE:
A single line of code is displayed like this:

This is an \textbf{example}.

Input

The corresponding output is illustrated like this:

This is an **example**.

Output

Segments of code that are longer than one line are bounded above and below, illustrated as follows:

[1.1] http://www.tex.ac.uk/faq

Input ⊤

```
Line one\par
Line two\par
Line three.
```

Input ⊥

with corresponding output:

Output ⊤

Line one
Line two
Line three.

Output ⊥

Command definitions are shown in a typewriter font in the form:

Definition   `\documentclass[⟨options⟩]{⟨class file⟩}`

In this case the command being defined is called `\documentclass` and text typed ⟨*like this*⟩ (such as ⟨*options*⟩ and ⟨*class file*⟩) indicates the type of thing you need to substitute. (Don't type the angle brackets!) For example, if you want the scrbook class file you would substitute ⟨*class file*⟩ with `scrbook` and if you want the `letterpaper` option you would substitute ⟨*options*⟩ with `letterpaper`, like this:

Input   `\documentclass[letterpaper]{scrbook}`

When it's important to indicate a space, the visible space symbol ␣ is used. For example:

Input   `A␣sentence␣consisting␣of␣six␣words.`

When you type up the code, replace any occurrences of ␣ with a space.

⚠ **NOTE:**

Be careful of the dangers of obsolete code propagation. It often happens that students pass on their LaTeX code to new students who, in their turn, pass it on to the next lot of students, and so on. You're told "use this magic bit of code to format your thesis" without knowing what it does. Ancient buggy code that's 20 years out-of-date festers in university departments refusing to die. But if it worked for previous students, what's the problem? The problem is that it may stop working a week before your submission date and when you go for help, you may be told you're using obsolete packages and there's nothing for it but to rewrite your thesis using the modern alternatives.

How do you know if a package is obsolete? Some of the obsolete packages and commands are listed in l2tabu [18], or you can check to see if a package is listed in the Comprehensive TeX Archive Network[1.2] (CTAN)'s obsolete tree (http://mirror.ctan.org/obsolete/). Stefan Kottwitz also has a list of obsolete classes

---

[1.2] http://mirror.ctan.org/

and packages in his TeXblog[1.3]. The other thing to do is check the package's entry on CTAN [2] to see if it has been deprecated. For example, suppose someone tells you to use the glossary package. If you go to `http://ctan.org/pkg/glossary` it will tell you that the glossary package is no longer supported and that it's been replaced by the glossaries package. Similarly, if you go to `http://ctan.org/pkg/epsfig` it will tell you that the epsfig package is obsolete and you should use graphicx instead.

1.1. Building Your Document

To "typeset", "build", "compile" or "LaTeX" your document means to run the `pdflatex` (or `latex`) executable on your document source code. If you are using a front-end, such as TeXworks, WinEdt, TeXstudio, or TeXnicCenter, this usually just means clicking on the appropriate button or selecting the appropriate menu item. (See Volume 1 [15, §3] for further details.)

It's important to remember that a front-end is an *interface*. It's not, for example, TeXworks that is creating your PDF. When you click on the "typeset" button, TeXworks tells the operating system to run the required executable. This is usually `pdflatex`, but there are other executables that may need to be used to help create your document, such as `bibtex` or `biber` (discussed in Chapter 5 (Generating a Bibliography)) and `makeindex` or `xindy` (discussed in Chapter 6 (Generating Indexes and Glossaries)).

For example, if your document has a bibliography and you are using TeXworks, you first need to make sure the drop-down menu is set to "pdfLaTeX" (see Figure 1.1 on the following page) and click on the green "Typeset" button. Then you need to select "BibTeX" from the drop-down menu (see Figure 1.2 on the next page) and click on the green "Typeset" button. Then again select "pdfLaTeX" (Figure 1.1 on the following page) and click the "Typeset" button. Finally, to ensure your cross-references are all up-to-date, you need to click on the "Typeset" button again. If you are using `biber` instead of `bibtex` (see Section 5.3), then you have to replace the above "BibTeX" step with "Biber" instead.

If the tool you require isn't listed in the drop-down box, you will have to add it. For example, to add `makeglossaries` to the list of available tools in TeXworks, you need to select Edit→Preferences, which will open the "TeXworks Preferences" dialog. Make sure the "Typesetting" tab is selected and click on the lower + button next to the "Processing tools" list. This will open the "Tool Configuration" dialog. Set the "Name" field to the name of the application, as you want it to appear in the tool list (for example "MakeGlossaries"). Then click on the "Browse" button to find the application on your computer. Next you need to click on the + button next to the "Arguments" list. Set the argument to `$basename`. Since `makeglossaries` doesn't modify the PDF, uncheck the "View PDF after running" box (see Figure 1.3 on page 5).

This is a bit of a hassle (if not downright confusing for a beginner) and even more so when you have glossaries and an index in your document as well as a bibliography. Fortunately there are ways of automating this process so that you only need one

---

[1.3] `http://texblog.net/latex-articles/packages/`

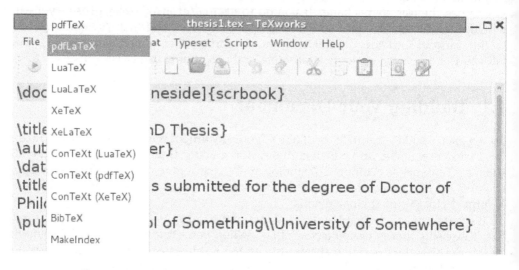

Figure 1.1. Selecting pdfLaTeX from the Drop-Down Menu

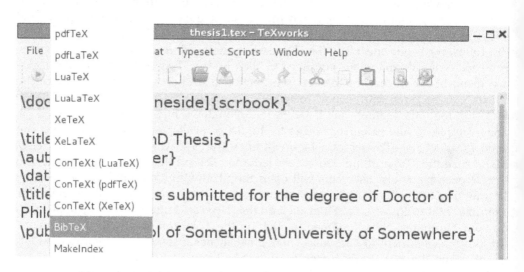

Figure 1.2. Selecting BibTeX from the Drop-Down Menu

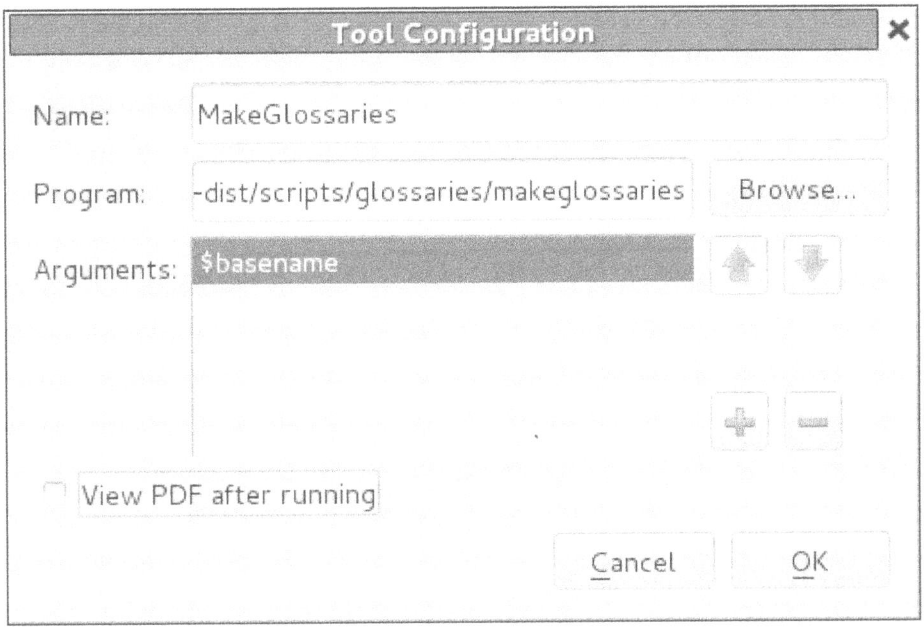

Figure 1.3. Adding Makeglossaries to the list of tools in TeXworks

button press to perform all those different steps. There are several applications available to do this for you, and I strongly recommend you try one of them, if possible, to reduce the complexity involved in building a document.

Volume 1 [15, §5.5] mentioned `latexmk`, which is available on CTAN [2]. This is a Perl script, so it will run on any operating system that has Perl installed (see Volume 1 [15, §2.20]). Since Volume 1 was published, a Java alternative called `arara` has arrived on CTAN [2]. Java applications will run on any operating system that has the Java Runtime Environment[1.4] installed, so both `latexmk` and `arara` are multi-platform solutions to automated document compilation. Section 1.1.1 gives a brief introduction to `latexmk`, and Section 1.1.2 gives a brief introduction to `arara`.

1.1.1. LaTeXmk

As mentioned above, `latexmk` is a Perl script that automates the process of building a LaTeX document. In order to use `latexmk`, you must have Perl installed (see Volume 1 [15, §2.20]). Both TeX Live and MikTeX come with `latexmk` but, if for some reason you don't have it installed, you can use the TeX Live or MikTeX update manager to install it. Alternatively, you can download `http://mirror.ctan.org/support/latexmk.zip` and install it manually.

Once `latexmk` is installed, you then need to add it to the list of available tools in

---

[1.4]`http://www.java.com/getjava/`

TeXworks[1.5]. This is done via the Edit→Preferences menu item. This opens TeXwork's Preferences dialog box. Make sure the "Typesetting" tab is selected (Figure 1.4).

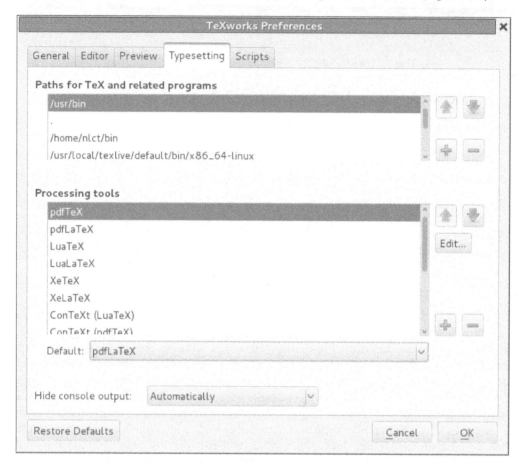

Figure 1.4. TeXwork's Preferences Dialog Box

To add a new tool, click on the lower ⊞ button next to the list of processing tools. This opens the tool configuration dialog box (Figure 1.5 on the next page).

Type "LaTeXmk" in the "Name" box, then use the "Browse" button to locate latexmk on your computer. Next you need to click on the ⊞ button to add each argument. The argument list should consist of the following (in the order listed):

```
-e
$pdflatex=q/pdflatex $synctexoption %O %S/
-pdf
-bibtex
$fullname
```

[1.5]If you are using a different front-end, you will have to consult your front-end's manual.

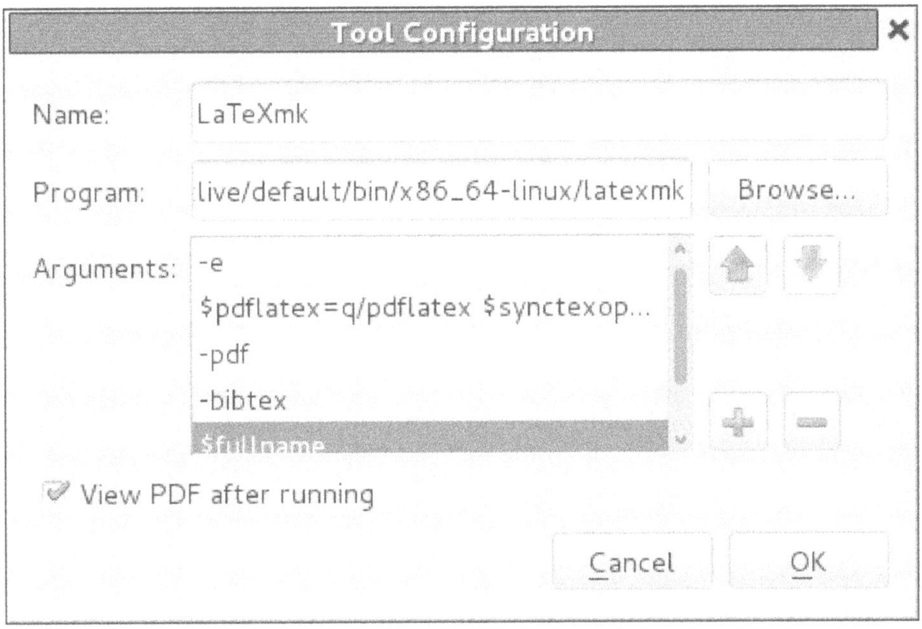

Figure 1.5. Adding LaTeXmk in the TeXWorks Tool Configuration Dialog

Once you've done this, click "Okay" to close the tool configuration dialog, and click "Okay" to close the Preferences dialog box. LaTeXmk should now be listed in the drop-down menu next to the green "Typeset" button. Now, if you have LaTeXmk selected and you click on the "Typeset" button `pdflatex` and `bibtex`/`biber` will be run as necessary to create an up-to-date PDF.

Unfortunately, adding `makeindex`, `texindy` or `makeglossaries` to LaTeXmk's set of rules is more complicated. For this you need to create a configuration/initialisation (RC) file[1.6]. The name and location of this file depends on your operating system. For example, on a Unix-like operating system, this may be `$HOME/.latexmkrc`. You will need to consult the `latexmk` manual [1] for further details.

Once you've found out the name and location of the RC file for your operating system, you can use the text editor of your choice to create this file. To add `makeglossaries`, you need to type the following in the RC file:

```
add_cus_dep('glo', 'gls', 0, 'makeglossaries');
add_cus_dep('acn', 'acr', 0, 'makeglossaries');
sub makeglossaries{
  system( "makeglossaries \"$_[0]\"" );
}
```

To add `makeindex`, you need to type the following:

[1.6]There are some example RC files available at: `http://mirror.ctan.org/support/latexmk/example_rcfiles/`.

```
add_cus_dep('idx', 'ind', 0, 'makeindex');
sub makeindex{
  system("makeindex \"$_[0].idx\"");
}
```

If you prefer to use `texindy` instead of `makeindex`, you will need to replace the above lines with (change the language as appropriate):

```
add_cus_dep('idx', 'ind', 0, 'texindy');
sub texindy{
  system("texindy -L english \"$_[0].idx\"");
}
```

Now select "LaTeXmk" from the drop-down menu next to the green "Typeset" button in TeXworks (Figure 1.6 on the facing page), and you're ready to build your documents.

1.1.2. Arara

As mentioned in Section 1.1, arara is a Java application that automates the process of building a LaTeX document. In order to use arara, you must have the Java Runtime Environment installed. The latest TeX Live distribution includes arara, so you can install it via the TeX Live package manager.

Alternative, you can install arara manually as follows: fetch the installer `arara-3.0 -installer.jar` (or `arara-3.0-installer.exe`) from `https://github.com/cereda/ arara/tree/master/releases`. On Windows, run `arara-3.0-installer.exe`. On other operating systems run `arara-3.0-installer.jar` in privileged mode. For example, on a Unix-based system:

```
sudo java -jar arara-3.0-installer.jar
```

(If you are doing a manual install make sure you check the box to add the predefined rules, as shown in Figure 1.7 on page 10.)

Once arara has been installed, you can add it to the list of tools in TeXworks. As before, open the TeXwork's Preferences dialog box using Edit→Preferences and select the "Typesetting" tab (Figure 1.4 on page 6).

To add a new tool, click on the lower ✦ button next to the list of processing tools. This opens the tool configuration dialog box (Figure 1.8 on page 11). Type "Arara" in the "Name" box and use the "Browse" button to find the arara application on your computer. Use the ✦ button to add $basename to the list of arguments, as shown in Figure 1.8 on page 11.

Unlike `latexmk`, arara doesn't read the log file to determine what applications need to be run. Instead, you tell arara how to build your document by placing special comments in your source code. For example, if your document contains the following:

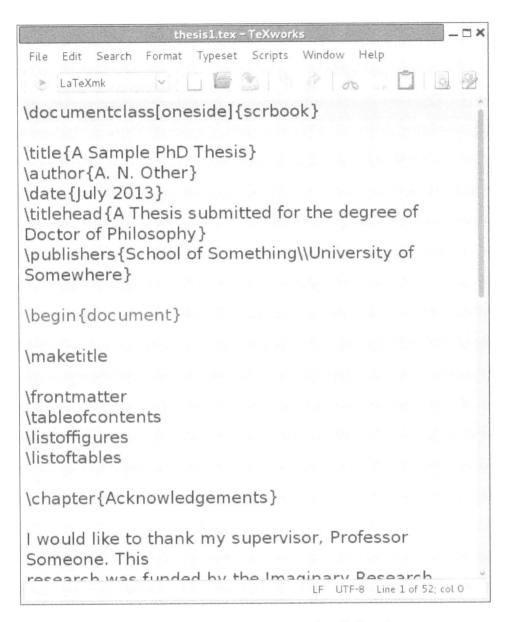

Figure 1.6. LaTeXmk Tool Selected in TeXworks

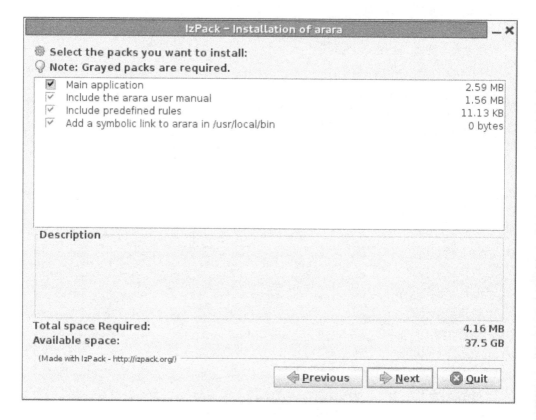

Figure 1.7. Arara Installer

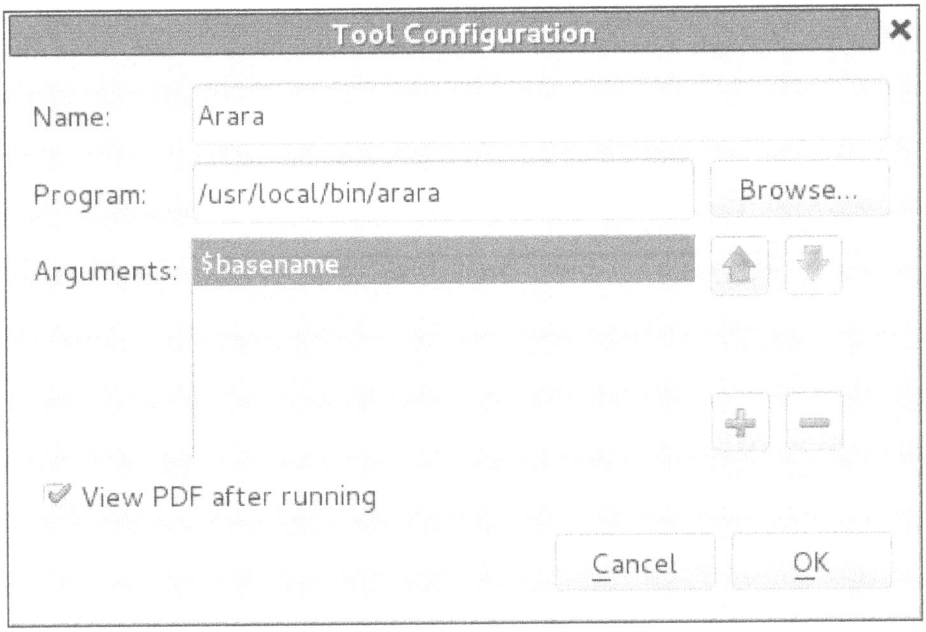

Figure 1.8. Adding Arara in the TeXWorks Tool Configuration Dialog

↑ Input

```
% arara: pdflatex: { synctex: on }
% arara: bibtex
% arara: pdflatex: { synctex: on }
% arara: pdflatex: { synctex: on }
\documentclass{scrbook}
```

↓ Input

Then running arara on the document will run pdflatex, bibtex, pdflatex and pdflatex on your document. Arara knows the rules "pdflatex" and "bibtex". It also knows the rules "biber", "makeglossaries" and "makeindex". So, if your document has a bibliography, an index and glossaries, you need to put the following comments in your source code (replace bibtex with biber if required):

↑ Input

```
% arara: pdflatex: { synctex: on }
% arara: bibtex
% arara: makeglossaries
% arara: makeindex
% arara: pdflatex: { synctex: on }
% arara: pdflatex: { synctex: on }
\documentclass{scrbook}
```

↓ Input

Now you just need to select "Arara" from the drop-down list in TeXworks (Figure 1.9 on the next page) and click the green "Typeset" button, and arara will do all the work for you.

NOTE:

If you don't add these arara comments to your source code, nothing will happen when you run arara on your document! You must remember to provide arara with the rules to build your document.

Unfortunately arara (v3.0) doesn't have a rule for texindy, but you can add one by creating a file called texindy.yaml that contains the following:[1.7]

```
!config
# TeXindy rule for arara
# requires arara 3.0+
identifier: texindy
name: TeXindy
command: <arara> texindy @{german} @{language} @{codepage} @{module}
@{input} @{options} "@{getBasename(file)}.idx"          ↩
arguments:
- identifier: german
  flag: <arara> @{isTrue(parameters.german,"-g")}
- identifier: language
  flag: <arara> -L @{parameters.language}
- identifier: codepage
  flag: <arara> -C @{parameters.codepage}
- identifier: module
  flag: <arara> -M @{parameters.module}
- identifier: input
  flag: <arara> -I @{parameters.input}
- identifier: options
  flag: <arara> @{parameters.options}
```

(The symbol ↩ above indicates a line wrap. Don't insert a line break at that point.) This file should be saved in the rules subdirectory of the arara installation directory. (For example, on Unix-like systems /usr/local/arara/rules/texindy.yaml.)

So if you'd rather use texindy instead of makeindex you can replace the

```
% arara: makeindex
```

directive with

```
% arara: texindy: { language: english, codepage: latin1 }
```

(Change the language and encoding as appropriate.)

[1.7]Thanks to Paulo Cereda for supply this.

Figure 1.9. Using Arara in TeXworks

Chapter 2

Getting Started

There are many different thesis designs, varying according to university or discipline [5]. If you have been told to use a particular class file, use that one. If not, there are a selection of thesis class files available on CTAN [2] and listed in the OnLine TeX Catalogue's Topic Index[2.1] [3]. Since there are so many to choose from, I'm just going to follow on from Volume 1 of this series and use one of the KOMA-Script class files. But which one? The scrreprt class is the one usually recommended for a report or thesis. It defaults to one-sided and has an abstract environment, but it doesn't define \frontmatter, \mainmatter or \backmatter. The scrbook class does define those commands, but it doesn't provide an abstract environment and defaults to two-sided layout. So, you can either do:

↑ Input

```
\documentclass{scrreprt}
\title{A Sample Thesis}
\author{A.N. Other}

\begin{document}
\maketitle

\pagenumbering{roman}
\tableofcontents

\chapter*{Acknowledgements}

\begin{abstract}
This is the abstract
\end{abstract}

\pagenumbering{arabic}

\chapter{Introduction}
...
\end{document}
```

↓ Input

[2.1]http://mirror.ctan.org/help/Catalogue/bytopic.html#theses

or you can do:

Input ⊤

```
\documentclass[oneside]{scrbook}
\title{A Sample Thesis}
\author{A.N. Other}

\begin{document}
\maketitle

\frontmatter
\tableofcontents

\chapter{Acknowledgements}

\chapter{Abstract}
This is the abstract

\mainmatter

\chapter{Introduction}
...
\end{document}
```

Input ↓

I'm going to use the second approach simply out of personal preference. The KOMA-Script options mentioned in this book are available for both scrreprt and scrbook, so choose whichever class file you feel best suits your thesis.

Unless you have been told otherwise, I recommend that you start out with a skeletal document that looks something like the following:

Input ⊤

Listing 1[2.2]

```
\documentclass[oneside]{scrbook}

\title{A Sample Thesis}
\author{A.N. Other}
\date{July 2013}
\titlehead{A Thesis submitted for the degree of Doctor of Philosophy}
\publishers{School of Something\\University of Somewhere}

\begin{document}
\maketitle
```

[2.2]http://www.dickimaw-books.com/latex/thesis/html/examples/thesis1.tex

```
\frontmatter
\tableofcontents
\listoffigures
\listoftables

\chapter{Acknowledgements}

I would like to thank my supervisor, Professor Someone. This
research was funded by the Imaginary Research Council.

\chapter{Abstract}

A brief summary of the project goes here.

% A glossary and list of acronyms may go here
% or may go in the back matter.

\mainmatter

\chapter{Introduction}
\label{ch:intro}

\chapter{Technical Introduction}
\label{ch:techintro}

\chapter{Method}
\label{ch:method}

\chapter{Results}
\label{ch:results}

\chapter{Conclusions}
\label{ch:conc}

\backmatter

% A glossary and list of acronyms may go here
% or may go in the front matter after the abstract.

% The bibliography will go here

\end{document}
```

⤓ Input

If you do this, it will help ensure that your document has the correct structure
before you begin with the actual contents of the document. (Note that the chapter

titles will naturally vary depending on your subject or institution, and you may need a different paper size if you are not in Europe. I have based the above on my own PhD thesis which I wrote in the early to mid 1990s in the Department of Electronic Systems Engineering at the University of Essex, and it may well not fit your own requirements.)

If you haven't started your thesis yet, go ahead and try this. Creating a skeletal document can have an amazing psychological effect on some people: for very little effort it can produce a document several pages long, which can give you a sense of achievement that can help give you sufficient momentum to get started (but of course, it's not guaranteed to work with everyone). Remember that if you want to use arara (see Section 1.1.2) you must add the build rules to the document:

Input ↑
```
% arara: pdflatex: { synctex: on }
% arara: pdflatex: { synctex: on }
\documentclass[oneside]{scrbook}
```
Input ↓

(I'll add the arara rules to sample listings, in the event that you want to use arara. Since they are comments, they will be ignored if you use pdflatex explicitly or if you use another automation method, such as latexmk.)

Now think about other requirements. What font size have you been told to use?

10pt Use the 10pt class option:

Input
```
\documentclass[oneside,10pt]{scrbook}
```

11pt Use the 11pt class option:

Input
```
\documentclass[oneside,11pt]{scrbook}
```

12pt Use the 12pt class option:

Input
```
\documentclass[oneside,12pt]{scrbook}
```

Have you been told to have a blank line between paragraphs and no paragraph indentation? If so, use the parskip=full class option:

Input
```
\documentclass[oneside,12pt,parskip=full]{scrbook}
```

[FAQ: Changing the margins in LATEX] Have you been told to have certain sized margins? If so, you can use the geometry package. For example, if you have been told you must have 1 inch margins, you can do

Input
```
\usepackage[margin=1in]{geometry}
```

Changing the default fonts is covered in Volume 1 [15, §4.5.3]. Other possible formatting requirements, such as double-spacing, are covered in Chapter 4 (Formatting).

CHAPTER 3

SPLITTING A LARGE DOCUMENT INTO SEVERAL FILES

Some people prefer to place each chapter of a large document in a separate file and then input the file into the main document.

There are two basic ways of including the contents of an external file:

\input{⟨*filename*⟩}   Definition

and

\include{⟨*filename*⟩}   Definition

where ⟨*filename*⟩ is the name of the file. (The .tex extension may be omitted in both cases.) The differences between the two commands are as follows:

\input acts as though the contents of the file were typed where the \input command was. For example, suppose my main file contained the following:

```
Here is a short paragraph.

\input{myfile}
```

and suppose the file myfile.tex contained the following lines:

```
Here is some sample text.
```

then the \input command behaves as though you had simply typed the following in your main document file:

19

Input ⊤

> Here is a short paragraph.
>
> Here is some sample text.

Input ⊥

\include does more than just input the contents of the file. It also starts a new page (using \clearpage) and creates an auxiliary file associated with the included file. It also issues another \clearpage once the file has been read in. Using this approach, you can also govern which files to include using

Definition

\includeonly{⟨*file list*⟩}

in the preamble, where ⟨*file list*⟩ is a comma-separated list of files you want included. This way, if you only want to work on one or two chapters, you can only include those chapters, which will speed up the document build. LaTeX will still read in all the cross-referencing information for the missing chapters, but won't include those chapters in the PDF file. There is a definite advantage to this if you have, say, a large number of images in your results chapter, which you don't need when you're working on, say, the technical introduction. You can still reference all the figures in the omitted chapter, as long as you have previously LaTeXed the document without the \includeonly command.

The excludeonly package provides the logically opposite command:

Definition

\excludeonly{⟨*file list*⟩}

The previous example on page 16 can now be split into various files:

Input ⊤

Listing 2 (thesis.tex)[3.1]

```
% arara: pdflatex: { synctex: on }
% arara: pdflatex: { synctex: on }
\documentclass[oneside]{scrbook}

\title{A Sample Thesis}
\author{A.N. Other}
\date{July 2013}
\titlehead{A Thesis submitted for the degree of Doctor of Philosophy}
\publishers{School of Something\\University of Somewhere}

\begin{document}
```

[3.1]http://www.dickimaw-books.com/latex/thesis/html/examples/thesis2.tex

```
\maketitle

\frontmatter
\tableofcontents
\listoffigures
\listoftables

\chapter{Acknowledgements}

I would like to thank my supervisor, Professor Someone. This
research was funded by the Imaginary Research Council.

\chapter{Abstract}

A brief summary of the project goes here.

\mainmatter

\include{intro}

\include{techintro}

\include{method}

\include{results}

\include{conc}

\backmatter

\end{document}
```

↓ Input

Listing 3 (`intro.tex`)[3.2]

↑ Input

```
\chapter{Introduction}
\label{ch:intro}
```

↓ Input

Listing 4 (`techintro.tex`)[3.3]

↑ Input

```
\chapter{Technical Introduction}
\label{ch:techintro}
```

↓ Input

[3.2]http://www.dickimaw-books.com/latex/thesis/html/examples/intro.tex
[3.3]http://www.dickimaw-books.com/latex/thesis/html/examples/techintro.tex

Input ⊤ — Listing 5 (`method.tex`)[3.4]

```
\chapter{Method}
\label{ch:method}
```

Input ⊥

Input ⊤ — Listing 6 (`results.tex`)[3.5]

```
\chapter{Results}
\label{ch:results}
```

Input ⊥

Input ⊤ — Listing 7 (`conc.tex`)[3.6]

```
\chapter{Conclusions}
\label{ch:conc}
```

Input ⊥

If you only want to work on, say, the Method and Results chapters, you can place the following command in the preamble:

Input   `\includeonly{method,results}`

[3.4]http://www.dickimaw-books.com/latex/thesis/html/examples/method.tex
[3.5]http://www.dickimaw-books.com/latex/thesis/html/examples/results.tex
[3.6]http://www.dickimaw-books.com/latex/thesis/html/examples/conc.tex

CHAPTER 4

FORMATTING

It used to be that in order to change the format of chapter and section headings, you needed to have some understanding of the internal workings of classes such as report or book. Modern classes, such as memoir and the KOMA-Script classes, provide a much easier interface. However, I recommend that you first write your thesis, and then worry about changing the document style. The ability to separate content from style is one of the advantages of using LaTeX over a word processor. Remember that writing your thesis is more important than the layout. Whilst it may be that your school or department insists on a certain style, it should not take precedence over the actual task of writing.

4.1. Changing the Document Style

If you are using a custom thesis class file provided by your department or school, then you should stick to the styles set up in that class. If not, you may need to change the default style of your chosen class to fit the requirements. Volume 1 [15, §5.3] described how to change the fonts used by chapter and section headings for the KOMA-Script classes. For example, if the chapter headings must be set in a large, bold, serif font you can do:

`\addtokomafont{\large\bfseries\rmfamily}` *Input*

The headings in the KOMA-Script classes default to ragged-right justification (recall `\raggedright` from §2.12 of Volume 1) which is done via

`\raggedsection` *Definition*

This can be redefined as required. For example, suppose you are required to have centred headings, then you can do:

`\renewcommand*{\raggedsection}{\centering}` *Input*

4.2. Changing the Page Style

Volume 1 [15, §5.7] described the command

`\pagestyle{⟨style⟩}` *Definition*

23

which can be used to set the page style. The scrbook class defaults to the headings page style, but if this isn't appropriate, you can use the scrpage2 package, which comes with the KOMA-Script bundle. This package provides its own versions of the plain and headings page styles, called scrplain and scrheadings.

For simplicity, I'm assuming that your thesis is a one-sided document. If this isn't the case and your odd and even page styles need to be different, you'll need to consult the KOMA-Script documentation [8].

With the scrheadings page style, the page header and footer are both divided into three areas (Figure 4.1): the inner (left) head/foot, the centre head/foot and the outer (right) head/foot.

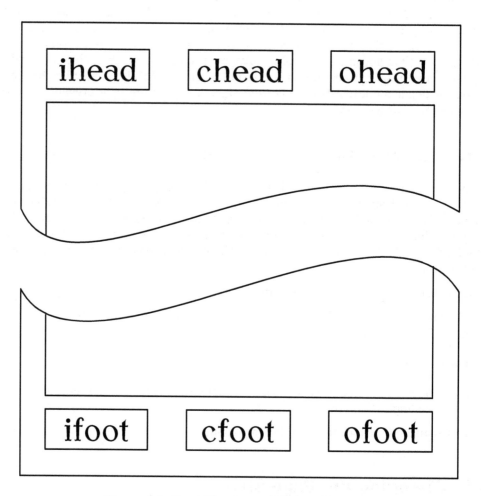

Figure 4.1. Page Header and Footer Elements

These elements can be set using:

\ihead[⟨*scrplain inner head*⟩]{⟨*scrheadings inner head*⟩}
\chead[⟨*scrplain centre head*⟩]{⟨*scrheadings centre head*⟩}
\ohead[⟨*scrplain outer head*⟩]{⟨*scrheadings outer head*⟩}
\ifoot[⟨*scrplain inner foot*⟩]{⟨*scrheadings inner foot*⟩}   Definition
\cfoot[⟨*scrplain centre foot*⟩]{⟨*scrheadings centre foot*⟩}
\ofoot[⟨*scrplain outer foot*⟩]{⟨*scrheadings outer foot*⟩}

In each case, the optional argument indicates what to do if the scrplain page style
is in use and the mandatory argument indicates what to do if the scrheadings page
style is in use. (If the optional argument is missing, no modification is made to the
scrplain style.) Within both types of argument, you can use

\pagemark   Definition

to insert the current page number and

\headmark   Definition

to insert the running heading. For example, suppose you are required to put your
registration number on the bottom left of each page and the page number on the
bottom right, and you are also required to put the current chapter or section heading
at the top left of each page, unless it's the first page of a chapter. Then you can do:

Listing 8[4.1]   ↑ Input

```
\usepackage{scrpage2}

\pagestyle{scrheadings}

\newcommand{\myregnum}{123456789}% registration number

\ihead{}
\chead{}
\ohead[]{\headmark}
\ifoot[\myregnum]{\myregnum}% registration number
\cfoot[]{}
\ofoot[\pagemark]{\pagemark}
```
                                                                               ↓ Input

Note that the above don't use any font changing commands. If you want to
change the font for the header and footer, you need to redefine \headfont. The
page number style is given by \pnumfont. So for italic headers and footers with bold
page numbers, you can redefine these commands as follows:

[4.1]http://www.dickimaw-books.com/latex/thesis/html/examples/thesis-pagestyles.tex

Input ↑
Input ↓

```
\renewcommand*{\headfont}{\normalfont\itshape}
\renewcommand*{\pnumfont}{\normalfont\bfseries}
```

4.3. Double-Spacing

Whilst double-spacing is usually frowned upon in the world of modern typesetting, it is usually a requirement for anything that may need hand-written annotations, which can include theses. This extra space gives the examiners room to write comments.[4.2]

Double-spacing can be achieved via the setspace package. You can either set the spacing using the package options singlespacing, onehalfspacing or doublespacing, or you can switch via the declarations:

Definition
```
\singlespacing
\onehalfspacing
\doublespacing
```

So, if your thesis has to be double-spaced, you can do:

Listing 9[4.3]

Input ↑
Input ↓

```
\usepackage[doublespacing]{setspace}
```

4.4. Changing the Title Page

Volume 1 [15, §5.1] described how to lay out the title page using \maketitle. If this layout isn't appropriate for your school or department's specifications, you can lay out the title page manually using the titlepage environment instead of \maketitle. Within this environment, you can use \hspace{⟨*length*⟩} and \vspace{⟨*length*⟩} to insert horizontal and vertical spacing. (The unstarred versions are ignored if they occur at the start of a line or page, respectively. The starred versions will insert the given spacing, regardless of their location.) You can also use \hfill and \vfill, which will expand to fill the available space horizontally or vertically, respectively.

[4.2]Despite the current digital age, many people still use hand-written annotations on manuscripts. It's unlikely that your examiners have pens that are incompatible with your paper.

[4.3]http://www.dickimaw-books.com/latex/thesis/html/examples/thesis-doublespaced.tex

EXAMPLE:

Listing 10[4.4]

↑ Input

```
\begin{titlepage}
 \centering
 \vspace*{1in}
 \begin{Large}\bfseries
  A Sample PhD Thesis\par
 \end{Large}
 \vspace{1.5in}
 \begin{large}\bfseries
  A. N. Other\par
 \end{large}
 \vfill
 A Thesis submitted for the degree of Doctor of Philosophy
 \par
 \vspace{0.5in}
 School of Something
 \par
 University of Somewhere
 \par
 \vspace{0.5in}
 July 2013
 \par
\end{titlepage}
```

↓ Input

The result is shown in Figure 4.2 on the following page. (If you require double-spacing, you may need to wait until after the title page before switching to double-spacing.)

4.5. Listings and Other Verbatim Text

There may be times when you want to include text exactly as you have typed it into your source code. For example, you may want to include a short segment of computer code. This can be done using the verbatim environment.

[FAQ: Code listings in LaTeX]

EXAMPLE.
Note how I don't need to worry about special characters, such as #, within the verbatim environment:

[4.4]http://www.dickimaw-books.com/latex/thesis/html/examples/thesis-titlepage.tex

Figure 4.2. Sample Title Page

↑ Input

```
\begin{verbatim}
#include <stdio.h> /* needed for printf */

int main()
{
   printf("Hello World\n");

   return 1;
}
\end{verbatim}
```

↓ Input

This just produces:

↑ Output

```
#include <stdio.h> /* needed for printf */

int main()
{
   printf("Hello World\n");

   return 1;
}
```

↓ Output

A more sophisticated approach is to use the listings package. With this package, you first need to specify the programming language. For example, the above code is in C, so I need to specify this using:

```
\lstset{language=C}
```
Input

Now I can use the lstlisting environment to typeset my C code:

↑ Input

```
\begin{lstlisting}
#include <stdio.h> /* needed for printf */

int main()
{
   printf("Hello World\n");

   return 1;
}
\end{lstlisting}
```

↓ Input

The resulting output looks like:

Output ⊤

```
#include <stdio.h> /* needed for printf */

int main()
{
    printf("Hello World\n");

    return 1;
}
```

Output ⊥

I can also have inline code snippets using:

Definition   \lstinline[⟨*options*⟩]⟨*char*⟩⟨*code*⟩⟨*char*⟩

This is different syntax to the usual forms of command argument. You can chose
any character ⟨*char*⟩ that isn't the open square bracket [and that doesn't occur in
⟨*code*⟩ to delimit the code, but the start and end ⟨*char*⟩ must match. (The optional
argument is discussed below.) So the following are all equivalent:

    1. ⟨*char*⟩ is the exclamation mark character:

Input   `\lstinline!#include <stdio.h>!`

    2. ⟨*char*⟩ is the vertical bar character:

Input   `\lstinline|#include <stdio.h>|`

    3. ⟨*char*⟩ is the double-quote character:

Input   `\lstinline"#include <stdio.h>"`

    4. ⟨*char*⟩ is the plus symbol:

Input   `\lstinline+#include <stdio.h>+`

And so on, but ⟨*char*⟩ can't be, say, # as that occurs in ⟨*code*⟩. Example:

Input ⊤

```
The stdio header file (required for the \lstinline+printf+ function) is
loaded using the directive \lstinline!#include <stdio.h>! on the first
line.
```

Input ⊥

Result:

↑ Output

The stdio header file (required for the printf function) is loaded using the directive **#include** <stdio.h> on the first line.

↓ Output

Another alternative is to input the code from an external file. For example, suppose my C code is contained in the file `helloworld.c`, then I can input it using:

`\lstinputlisting[⟨options⟩]{helloworld.c}`

Input

(Remember to use a forward slash / as the directory divider, even if you are using Windows.)

All the above (`\lstinline`, `\lstinputlisting` and the lstlisting environment) have an optional argument ⟨*options*⟩ that can be used to override the default settings. These are ⟨*key*⟩=⟨*value*⟩ options. There are a lot of options available, but I'm only going to cover a few. If you want more detail, have a look at the listings documentation [6].

title={⟨*text*⟩} is used to set an unnumbered and unlabelled title. If ⟨*text*⟩ contains a comma or equal sign, make sure you enclose ⟨*text*⟩ in curly braces { and }.

caption={[⟨*short*⟩]⟨*text*⟩} is used to set a numbered caption. The optional part ⟨*short*⟩ is an alternative short caption for the list of listings, which can be produced using

`\lstlistoflistings`

Definition

As above, if the caption contains a comma or equal sign, make sure you enclose it in curly braces { and }.

label={⟨*text*⟩} is used to assign a label to this listing so the number can be referenced via `\ref`.

numbers={⟨*setting*⟩} The value ⟨*setting*⟩ may be one of: none (no line numbers), left (line numbers on the left) or right (line numbers on the right).

mathescape This is a boolean key that can either be true (dollar $ character acts as the usual math mode shift) or false (deactivates the usual behaviour of $).

basicstyle={⟨*declaration*⟩} The value (one or more declarations) is used at the start of the listing to set the basic font style. For example, ⟨*declaration*⟩ could be `\ttfamily` (which actually makes more sense for a listing).

NOTE:

If you set **basicstyle** to `\ttfamily` and you want bold keywords, make sure you are using a typewriter font that supports bold, as not all of them do. (Recall from Volume 1 [15, §4.5.3] how to change the font family.) This book uses txtt (see Volume 1 [15, §8.2]). Other possibilities include beramono, tgcursor, courier, DejaVuSansMono (or dejavu to load the serif and sans-serif DejaVu fonts as well), lmodern and luximono.

⚠ **KOMA AND listings**

If you want to use the listings package with one of the KOMA-Script classes, you need to load scrhack *before* listings, otherwise you will get a warning that looks like:

```
Class scrbook Warning: Usage of deprecated \float@listhead!
(scrbook)               You should use the features of package 'tocbasic'
(scrbook)               instead of \float@listhead.
(scrbook)               Definition of \float@listhead my be removed from
(scrbook)               'scrbook' soon, so it should not be used  on input
line 57.
```

EXAMPLE:

Input ⊤

Listing 11[4.5]

```
\begin{lstlisting}[language=C,basicstyle=\ttfamily,mathescape=true]
#include <stdio.h> /* needed for printf */
#include <math.h> /* needed for sqrt */

int main()
{
    double x = sqrt(2.0); /* $x = \sqrt{2}$ */

    printf("x = %f\n", x);

    return 1;
}
\end{lstlisting}
```

Input ⊥

Result:

Output ⊤

```
#include <stdio.h> /* needed for printf */
#include <math.h> /* needed for sqrt */

int main()
{
    double x = sqrt(2.0);  /* x = √2 */

    printf("x␣=␣%f\n", x);

    return 1;
}
```

Output ⊥

[4.5]http://www.dickimaw-books.com/latex/thesis/html/examples/thesis-listings.tex

If you are using double-spacing, you may need to temporarily switch it off in the listings. You can do this by adding \singlespacing to the basicstyle setting.

`\lstset{basicstyle={\ttfamily\singlespacing}}`   Input

(Check with your supervisor to find out if listings should be double- or single-spaced.)

NOTE:
It is not usually appropriate to have reams of listings in your thesis. It can annoy an examiner if you have included every single piece of code you have written during your PhD, as it comes across as padding to make it look as though your thesis is a lot larger than it really is. (Examiners are not easily fooled, and it's best not to irritate them as it is likely to make them less sympathetic towards you.) If you want to include listings in your thesis, check with your supervisor first to find out whether or not it is appropriate.

Be careful when you use verbatim-like environments or commands, such as verbatim, lstlisting, \lstinline and \lstinputlisting. In general, they can't be used in the argument of another command.

[FAQ: Why doesn't verbatim work within …?]

4.6. Tabbing

The tabbing environment lets you create tab stops so that you can tab to a particular distance from the left margin. Within the tabbing environment, you can use the command \= to set a tab stop, \> to jump to the next tab stop, \< to go back a tab stop, \+ to shift the left border by one tab stop to the right, \- to shift the left border by one tab stop to the left. In addition, \\ will start a new line and \kill will set any tabs stops defined in that line, but will not typeset the line itself.

NOTE:
You may recall two of the above commands from Volume 1: \- was described as a discretionary hyphen in §2.14 and \= was described as the macron accent command in §4.3. These two commands take on different meanings when they are used in the tabbing environment. If you want accents in your tabbing environment, either use the inputenc package (see Volume 1 [15, §4.3.1]) or use \a⟨*accent symbol*⟩{⟨c⟩}, for example \a"{u} instead of \"{u}.

[FAQ: Accents misbehave in tabbing]

EXAMPLE:

```
\begin{tabbing}
Zero \=One \=Two \=Three\\
\>First tab stop\\
\>A\>\>B\\
\>\>Second tab stop
\end{tabbing}
```
⊤ Input

↓ Input

This produces the following output:

Output ⊤

Zero One Two Three
    First tab stop
   A   B
      Second tab stop

Output ⊥

ANOTHER EXAMPLE:
This example sets up four tab stops, but ignores the first line:

Input ⊤

```
\begin{tabbing}
AAA \=BBBB \=XX \=YYYYYY \=Z \kill
\>\>\>Third tab stop\\
\>a \>b \> \>c
\end{tabbing}
```

Input ⊥

This produces the following output:

Output ⊤

          Third tab stop
   a   b   c

Output ⊥

4.7. Theorems

A PhD thesis can often contain theorems, lemmas, definitions etc. The LaTeX kernel comes with the command:

Definition   \newtheorem{⟨*name*⟩}[⟨*counter*⟩]{⟨*title*⟩}[⟨*outer counter*⟩]

which can be used to create an environment called ⟨*name*⟩ that has an optional argument. Each instance of the environment starts with ⟨*title*⟩ followed by the associated counter value. If ⟨*counter*⟩ is present, the new environment uses that counter instead of having a new counter defined for it. If ⟨*outer counter*⟩ is present, the environment counter is reset every time ⟨*outer counter*⟩ is incremented. The optional arguments are mutually exclusive.

In the example below, I've use \newtheorem to define a new environment called theorem, which has an associated counter, also called theorem, that is dependant on the chapter counter.

```
% in the preamble:
\newtheorem{theorem}{Theorem}[chapter]

% later in the document:
\begin{theorem}
If proposition $P$ is a tautology
then $\sim P$ is a contradiction,
and conversely.
\end{theorem}
```

↑ Input

↓ Input

Resulting output:

↑ Output

Theorem 4.1 *If proposition P is a tautology then ~ P is a contradiction, and conversely.*

↓ Output

The optional argument to the new environment can be used to add a caption. Modifying the above example (changes shown **like this**):

↑ Input

```
% in the preamble:
\newtheorem{theorem}{Theorem}[chapter]

% later in the document:
\begin{theorem}[Tautologies and Contradictions]
If proposition $P$ is a tautology
then $\sim P$ is a contradiction,
and conversely.
\end{theorem}
```

↓ Input

Resulting output:

↑ Output

Theorem 4.2 (Tautologies and Contradictions) *If proposition P is a tautology then ~ P is a contradiction, and conversely.*

↓ Output

Here's an example that uses the first optional argument of \newtheorem:

Input ↑

```
% in the preamble:
\newtheorem{exercise}{Exercise}
\newtheorem{suppexercise}[exercise]{Supplementary Exercise}

% later in the document:
\begin{exercise}
This is an example of how to create a theorem-like environment.
\end{exercise}
\begin{suppexercise}
This is another example of how to create a theorem-like environment.
\end{suppexercise}
```

Input ↓

Result:

Output ↑

Exercise 1 *This is an example of how to create a theorem-like environment.*

Supplementary Exercise 2 *This is another example of how to create a theorem-like environment.*

Output ↓

[FAQ: Theorem bodies printed in a roman font]

Unfortunately there isn't a great deal of flexibility with the environment appearance. However there are various packages available that provide enhancements to this basic command, allowing you to adjust the appearance to suit your requirements. There seem to be two main contenders: amsthm and ntheorem. Both have advantages and disadvantages. For example, ntheorem is more flexible but amsthm is more robust. Therefore I'm going to describe both, and you will have to decide which one you prefer.

⚠ **NOTE:**

If you are using either packages with amsmath, you must load amsmath first:

Input ↑

```
\usepackage{amsmath}
\usepackage{ntheorem}
```

Input ↓

or

Input ↑

```
\usepackage{amsmath}
\usepackage{amsthm}
```

Input ↓

With both amsthm and ntheorem, you can still define new theorem-like environments using \newtheorem, but there is also a starred version of that command, which can be used to define unnumbered theorem-like environments.

EXAMPLE:
Suppose I want to have an unnumbered remark environment, I can define the environment like this:

↑ Input

```
% in the preamble:
\newtheorem*{note}{Note}

% later in the document:
\begin{note}
This is a note about something.
\end{note}
```

↓ Input

Result:

↑ Output

Note *This is a note about something.*

↓ Output

4.7.1. The amsthm Package

The amsthm package provides three predefined theorem styles: plain, definition and remark. When you define a new theorem-like environment with \newtheorem, it is given the style *currently in effect*. You can change the current style with:

\theoremstyle{⟨*style name*⟩}   Definition

where ⟨*style name*⟩ is the name of the theorem style.

EXAMPLE:
This example defines six theorem-like environments: theorem, lemma, defn, conj, note and remark. The note environment is unnumbered as it's defined using the starred version of \newtheorem. The definitions have been arranged according to the required theorem style.

↑ Input

```
\theoremstyle{plain}
\newtheorem{theorem}{Theorem}
\newtheorem{lemma}{Lemma}

\theoremstyle{definition}
\newtheorem{defn}{Definition}
\newtheorem{conj}{Conjecture}
```

```
\theoremstyle{remark}
\newtheorem*{note}{Note}
\newtheorem{remark}{Remark}
```

Input ↓

The amsthm package also provides the proof environment, which can be used for typesetting proofs.

Definition `\begin{proof}[`⟨*title*⟩`]`

The optional argument ⟨*title*⟩ is a replacement for the default title. This environment automatically inserts a QED symbol at the end of it, but if the default location isn't appropriate (which can happen if the proof ends with an equation) then use

Definition `\qedhere`

where you want the QED symbol to appear. The symbol is given by

Definition `\qedsymbol`

This defaults to an unfilled square □, but you can redefine `\qedsymbol` to something else if you prefer. (Recall redefining commands from Volume 1 [15, §8.2].)

Input ↑

Listing 12[4.6]

```
% in the preamble:

\usepackage{amsthm}
\theoremstyle{plain}
\newtheorem{theorem}{Theorem}

\theoremstyle{definition}
\newtheorem{defn}{Definition}
\newtheorem{xmpl}{Example}[chapter]

\theoremstyle{remark}
\newtheorem{remark}{Remark}

% later in the document:

\begin{defn}[Tautology]\label{def:tautology}
A \emph{tautology} is a proposition that is always true for any value of
its variables.
\end{defn}

\begin{defn}[Contradiction]\label{def:contradiction}
```

[4.6]http://www.dickimaw-books.com/latex/thesis/html/examples/thesis-amsthm.tex

```
A \emph{contradiction} is a proposition that is always false for any
value of its variables.
\end{defn}

\begin{theorem}
If proposition $P$ is a tautology then $\sim P$ is a contradiction, and
conversely.
\begin{proof}
If $P$ is a tautology, then all elements of its truth table are true (by
Definition~\ref{def:tautology}), so all elements of the truth table for
$\sim P$ are false, therefore $\sim P$ is a contradiction (by
Definition~\ref{def:contradiction}).
\end{proof}
\end{theorem}

\begin{xmpl}\label{ex:rain}
``It is raining or it is not raining'' is a tautology, but ``it is not
raining and it is raining'' is a contradiction.
\end{xmpl}

\begin{remark}
Example~\ref{ex:rain} used De Morgan's Law $\sim (p \vee q) \equiv \sim p
\wedge \sim q$.
\end{remark}
```

↓ Input

Result:

↑ Output

Definition 1 (Tautology). A *tautology* is a proposition that is always true for any of its variables.

Definition 2 (Contradiction). A *contradiction* is a proposition that is always false for any value of its variables.

Theorem 4.3. *If proposition P is a tautology then $\sim P$ is a contradiction, and conversely.*

Proof. If P is a tautology, then all elements of its true table are true (by Definition 1), so all elements of the truth table for $\sim P$ are false, therefore $\sim P$ is a contradiction (by Definition 2). □

Example 1. "It is raining or it is not raining" is a tautology, but "it is not raining and it is raining" is a contradiction.

Remark 1. Example 1 used De Morgan's Law $\sim (p \vee q) \equiv \sim p \wedge \sim q$.

↓ Output

A new theorem style can be created using

\newtheoremstyle{⟨*name*⟩}{⟨*space above*⟩}{⟨*space below*⟩}{⟨*body font*⟩}{⟨*indent*⟩}{⟨*head font*⟩}{⟨*post head punctuation*⟩}{⟨*post head space*⟩}{⟨*head spec*⟩}

This defines a new theorem style called ⟨*name*⟩, which can later be set using \theoremstyle. The other arguments are as follows:

⟨*space above*⟩	the amount of space above the theorem-like environment
⟨*space below*⟩	the amount of space below the theorem-like environment
⟨*body font*⟩	the font to be used in the main theorem body
⟨*indent*⟩	the amount of indentation (empty means no indent or use \parindent for normal paragraph indentation)
⟨*head font*⟩	the font to be used in the theorem header
⟨*post head punctuation*⟩	the punctuation to be inserted after the theorem head
⟨*post head space*⟩	the space to put after the theorem head (use {␣} for a normal interword space or \newline for a linebreak)
⟨*head spec*⟩	the theorem head spec

EXAMPLE:
This example creates a new style called note that inserts a space of 2ex above the theorem and 2ex below.[4.7] The body font is just the normal font. There is no indent, the theorem header is in small caps, a full stop is put after the theorem head and a line break is inserted between the theorem head and body:

Input ⊤

```
\newtheoremstyle{note}% style name
{2ex}% above space
{2ex}% below space
{}% body font
{}% indent amount
{\scshape}% head font
{.}% post head punctuation
{\newline}% post head punctuation
{}% head spec
```

Input ⊥

Once you have defined the style, you can now use it. For example (in the preamble):

[4.7] Recall the ex unit from Volume 1 [15, §2.17].

↑ Input

```
\theoremstyle{note}
\newtheorem{scnote}{Note}
```

↓ Input

This defines a theorem-like environment called scnote. You can now use it later in the document:

↑ Input

```
\begin{scnote}
This is an example of a theorem-like environment.
\end{scnote}
```

↓ Input

This produces:

↑ Output

NOTE 1.

This is an example of a theorem-like environment.

↓ Output

4.7.2. The ntheorem Package

The ntheorem package provides nine predefined theorem styles, listed in Table 4.1. The default is plain. When you define a new theorem-like environment with \newtheorem, it is given the style *currently in effect*. You can change the current style with:

```
\theoremstyle{⟨style name⟩}
```

Definition

where ⟨*style name*⟩ is the name of the theorem style.

Table 4.1. Predefined Theorem Styles Provided by ntheorem

plain	Like the original LATEX style
break	Header is followed by a line break
change	Like plain but header and number interchanged
changebreak	Combination of change and break
margin	Number is set in the margin
marginbreak	Like margin but header followed by a line break
nonumberplain	Like plain but without the number
nonumberbreak	Like break but without the number
empty	No number and no name. Only the optional argument is used in the header.

In addition to these styles, you can also use

Definition `\theoremheaderfont{`⟨*declarations*⟩`}`

to set the header font to ⟨*declarations*⟩, which should consist of font declaration commands such as `\normalfont`,

Definition `\theorembodyfont{`⟨*declarations*⟩`}`

to set the body font to ⟨*declarations*⟩, and

Definition `\theoremnumbering{`⟨*style*⟩`}`

to set the appearance of the theorem number, where ⟨*style*⟩ may be one of: `arabic`, `roman`, `Roman`, `alph`, `Alph`, `greek`, `Greek` or `fnsymbol`. Remember that the above commands all need to be used before the new theorem-like environment is defined. For additional commands that affect the style of the theorems, see the ntheorem documentation [10].

EXAMPLE:

Input ↑

```
% in the preamble:
\theoremstyle{marginbreak}
\theorembodyfont{\normalfont}
\newtheorem{note}{Note}[chapter]

% later in the document:
\begin{note}
This is a sample note. The number is in the margin.
\end{note}
```

Input ↓

Result:

Output ↑

4.1 Note
This is a sample note. The number is in the margin.

Output ↓

If you use the `standard` package option to ntheorem, it will automatically define the following environments: Theorem, Lemma, Proposition, Corollary, Satz, Korollar, Definition, Example, Beispiel, Anmerkung, Bemerkung, Remark, Proof and Beweis.

 Unlike amsthm's proof environment, ntheorem's Proof environment appends its optional argument in parentheses, if present, to the proof title. (Recall from earlier on page 38 that amsthm's proof environment uses its optional argument as a replacement for the default proof title.)

EXAMPLE:

```
┌─ Listing 13⁴·⁸ ─────────────────────────────────────────────────┐   ↑ Input

% in the preamble:

\usepackage[standard]{ntheorem}

% later in the document:

\begin{Definition}[Tautology]\label{def:tautology}
A \emph{tautology} is a proposition that is always true for any value of
its variables.
\end{Definition}

\begin{Definition}[Contradiction]\label{def:contradiction}
A \emph{contradiction} is a proposition that is always false for any
value of its variables.
\end{Definition}

\begin{Theorem}
If proposition $P$ is a tautology then $\sim P$ is a contradiction, and
conversely.
\begin{Proof}
If $P$ is a tautology, then all elements of its truth table are true (by
Definition~\ref{def:tautology}), so all elements of the truth table for
$\sim P$ are false, therefore $\sim P$ is a contradiction (by
Definition~\ref{def:contradiction}).
\end{Proof}
\end{Theorem}

\begin{Example}\label{ex:rain}
``It is raining or it is not raining'' is a tautology, but ``it is not
raining and it is raining'' is a contradiction.
\end{Example}

\begin{Remark}
Example~\ref{ex:rain} used De Morgan's Law $\sim (p \vee q) \equiv \sim p
\wedge \sim q$.
\end{Remark}

└─────────────────────────────────────────────────────────────────┘   ↓ Input
```

Result:

---

⁴·⁸http://www.dickimaw-books.com/latex/thesis/html/examples/thesis-ntheorem.tex

Definition 3 (Tautology) A *tautology* is a proposition that is always true for any value of its variables.

Definition 4 (Contradiction) A *contradiction* is a proposition that is always false for any value of its variables.

Theorem 4.4 *If proposition P is a tautology then ∼ P is a contradiction, and conversely.*

PROOF If P is a tautology, then all elements of its truth table are true (by Definition 3), so all elements of the truth table for $\sim P$ are false, therefore $\sim P$ is a contradiction (by Definition 4).

Example 2 "It is raining or it is not raining" is a tautology, but "it is not raining and it is raining" is a contradiction.

Remark 2 Example 2 used De Morgan's Law $\sim (p \vee q) \equiv \sim p \wedge \sim q$.

4.8. Algorithms

If you want to display an algorithm, such as pseudo-code, you can use a combination of the tabbing environment (described in Section 4.6) and a theorem-like environment (described above in Section 4.7).

EXAMPLE:

```
% in the preamble:
\theoremstyle{break}
\theorembodyfont{\normalfont}
\newtheorem{algorithm}{Algorithm}

% later in the document:
\begin{algorithm}[Gauss-Seidel Algorithm]
\begin{tabbing}
1. \=For $k=1$ to maximum number of iterations\\
\>2. For \=$i=1$ to $n$\\
\>\>Set
\begin{math}
x_i^{(k)} =
\frac{b_i-\sum_{j=1}^{i-1}a_{ij}x_j^{(k)}
        -\sum_{j=i+1}^{n}a_{ij}x_j^{(k-1)}}}%
```

```
     {a_{ii}}
\end{math}
\\
\>3. If $\lvert\vec{x}^{(k)}-\vec{x}^{(k-1)}\rvert < \epsilon$,
where $\epsilon$ is a specified stopping criteria, stop.
\end{tabbing}
\end{algorithm}
```

⤓ Input

Result:

⤒ Output

Algorithm 1 (Gauss-Seidel Algorithm)
1. For $k = 1$ to maximum number of iterations
   2. For $i = 1$ to n
$$\text{Set } x_i^{(k)} = \frac{b_i - \sum_{j=1}^{i-1} a_{ij} x_j^{(k)} - \sum_{j=i+1}^{n} a_{ij} x_j^{(k-1)}}{a_{ii}}$$
3. If $|\vec{x}^{(k)} - \vec{x}^{(k-1)}| < \epsilon$, where ϵ is a specified stopping criteria, stop.

⤓ Output

(See Volume 1 [15, §9.4.11] to find out how to redefine \vec to display its argument in bold.)

If you want a more sophisticated approach, there are some packages available on CTAN [2], such as alg, algorithm2e, algorithms and algorithmicx. I'm going to briefly introduce the algorithm2e package here. This provides the algorithm floating environment. Like the figure and table environments described in Volume 1 [15, §7], the algorithm environment has an optional argument that specifies the placement.

```
\begin{algorithm}[⟨placement⟩]
```
Definition

If you are using a class or package that already defines an algorithm environment, you can use the algo2e package option:

```
\usepackage[algo2e]{algorithm2e}
```
Input

This will define an environment called algorithm2e instead of algorithm to avoid conflict.

Within the body of the environment, you must mark the end of each line with \; regardless of whether you want a semi-colon to appear. To suppress the default end-of-line semi-colon, use

```
\DontPrintSemicolon
```
Definition

To switch it back on again, use

```
\PrintSemicolon
```
Definition

There are a variety of commands that may be used within the algorithm environment. Some of the commands are described below, but for a complete list you should consult the algorithm2e documentation [4].

First there are the commands for the algorithm input, output and data:

Definition
```
\KwIn{⟨input⟩}
\KwOut{⟨output⟩}
\KwData{⟨input⟩}
\KwResult{⟨output⟩}
```

Next there are commands for basic keywords:

Definition
```
\KwTo
\KwRet{⟨value⟩}
\Return{⟨value⟩}
```

There are a lot of conditionals, but here's a selection:

Definition
```
\If{⟨condition⟩}{⟨then block⟩}
\uIf{⟨condition⟩}{⟨then block without end⟩}
\ElseIf{⟨else-if block⟩}
\uElseIf{⟨else-if block without end⟩}
\Else{⟨else block⟩}
```

Similarly there are a lot of loops, but here's a selection:

Definition
```
\For{⟨condition⟩}{⟨body⟩}
\While{⟨condition⟩}{⟨body⟩}
```

EXAMPLE:
The above algorithm can be written using the algorithm2e environment as follows (this document has used the algo2e package option):

Input
Listing 14[4.9]

```
\begin{algorithm2e}
\caption{Gauss-Seidel Algorithm}\label{alg:gauss-seidel}
\KwIn
{%
 scalar $\epsilon$,
 matrix $\mathbf{A} = (a_{ij})$,
 vector $\vec{b}$
 and initial vector $\vec{x}^{(0)}$
}
\For{$k\leftarrow 1$ \KwTo maximum iterations}
{
    \For{$i\leftarrow 1$ \KwTo $n$}
    {
        $
        x_i^{(k)} =
```

[4.9]http://www.dickimaw-books.com/latex/thesis/html/examples/thesis-algorithms.tex

```
    \frac
    {
      b_i-\sum_{j=1}^{i-1}a_{ij}x_j^{(k)}
      -\sum_{j=i+1}^{n}a_{ij}x_j^{(k-1)}
    }%
    {a_{ii}}
    $\;
  }
  \If{$\lvert\vec{x}^{(k)}-\vec{x}^{(k-1)}\rvert < \epsilon$}
  {Stop}
}
\end{algorithm2e}
```

↓ Input

The result is shown in Algorithm 2.

Input: Scalar ϵ, matrix $\mathbf{A} = (a_{ij})$, vector $\vec{b}$ and initial vector $\vec{x}^{(0)}$

for $k \leftarrow 1$ **to** *maximum iterations* **do**

    for $i \leftarrow 1$ **to** n **do**

        $x_i^{(k)} = \dfrac{b_i-\sum_{j=1}^{i-1}a_{ij}x_j^{(k)}-\sum_{j=i+1}^{n}a_{ij}x_j^{(k-1)}}{a_{ii}}$;

    end

    if $|\vec{x}^{(k)} - \vec{x}^{(k-1)}| < \epsilon$ **then**

        Stop

    end

end

Algorithm 2: Gauss-Seidel Algorithm

The algorithm environment (as defined by algorithm2e without the algo2e option) or algorithm2e environment (as defined with the algo2e option) uses the algocf counter. So in this document, to ensure that the algorithm environment defined with \newtheorem used the same counter as algorithm2e, I had the following in my preamble:

↑ Input

```
\usepackage{ntheorem}
\usepackage[algo2e]{algorithm2e}

\theoremstyle{break}
\theorembodyfont{\normalfont}
\newtheorem{algorithm}[algocf]{Algorithm}
```

↓ Input

4.9. Formatting SI Units

If you need to typeset numbers and units then I strongly recommend that you use the siunitx package. This section just provides a brief introduction to that package. You will need to read the siunitx package documentation [20] if you want further details.

Definition   \num{⟨*number*⟩}

This command typesets ⟨*number*⟩, adding appropriate spacing between number groups where necessary. It also adds a leading zero if omitted before the decimal point and identifies exponents. Note that the command recognises both "." and "," as the decimal marker. If you want one of these characters between number groups (instead of the default space) you can change the settings, but it's best to stick to the default settings unless instructed to do otherwise.

EXAMPLE:

Input ↑
```
Out of \num{12890} experiments, \num{1289} of them had a mean squared
error of \num{.346} and \num{128} of them had a mean squared error of
\num{1.23e-6}.
```
Input ↓

Result:

Output ↑
> Out of 12 890 experiments, 1289 of them had a mean squared error of 0.346 and 128 of them had a mean squared error of 1.23×10^{-6}.

Output ↓

Definition   \ang{⟨*angle*⟩}

This command typesets an angle. The argument ⟨*angle*⟩ may be a single number or three (some possibly empty) values separated by semi-colons.

EXAMPLE:

Input   `The result formed an arc from \ang{45} to \ang{60;2;3}.`

Result:

Output   The result formed an arc from 45° to 60°2′3″.

Definition   \si{⟨*unit*⟩}

This command typesets a unit. The ⟨*unit*⟩ can be formed from commands like \metre, \gram, \second or \kilo. (See the siunitx documentation [20] for the full list.)

EXAMPLE:

```
The distance was measured in \si{\kilo\metre} and the area in
\si{\kilo\metre\squared}. The acceleration was given in
\si{\metre\per\square\second}.
```

Result:

The distance was measured in km and the area in km². The acceleration was given in m s⁻².

$\SI{\langle number\rangle}{\langle unit\rangle}$ Definition

This combines the functionality of \num and \si so that you can typeset both a number and a unit.

EXAMPLE:

```
The acceleration was approximately \SI{9.78}{\metre\per\square\second}.
```

Result:

The acceleration was approximately $9.78\,\mathrm{m\,s^{-2}}$.   Output

CHAPTER 5

GENERATING A BIBLIOGRAPHY

Volume 1 [15, §5.6] introduced the thebibliography environment. While it is possible to write this environment yourself, as was done in Volume 1, it's not practical with a large number of citations.

Instead, the preferred method is to create an external database of bibliographic data and use an application that fetches the relevant information from that database and writes a file containing the thebibliography environment, which can then be input into your document. This means that:

1. Only the references that you cite are included in the bibliography. (Examiners tend to fault uncited references[5.1].)

2. References are displayed in a consistent manner.

3. Entries can be sorted in order of citation or alphabetically.

Traditionally the bibtex[5.2] application is used to generate the thebibliography environment. It comes with TeX distributions and most books on LaTeX cover bibtex. Unfortunately bibtex has some drawbacks, most notably the complexity of creating your own custom style. UTF-8 has also been a problem, although newer versions of bibtex apparently fix this.

In 2006, Philipp Lehman brought out the biblatex package to provide a more flexible way of typesetting bibliographies. This originally used bibtex to just sort the entries and used LaTeX macros to deal with the actual formatting, but it is now moving over to using biber[5.3] instead of bibtex.

Since some journals, conferences or other types of scientific publishers require you to use bibtex, Section 5.2 provides a brief introduction to bibtex and then Section 5.3 discusses biblatex and biber. But first Section 5.1 covers creating the actual database, which is required for both methods.

[5.1] When your examiners read through your thesis, they can check off each citation they encounter against your bibliography. When they reached the end of the thesis, they can then look through the bibliography for unchecked entries. One or two may appear the result of carelessness, whereas a large quantity will look like padding and may lead the examiners to suspect a certain amount of duplicity on your part.

[5.2] http://www.bibtex.org/

[5.3] http://biblatex-biber.sourceforge.net/

5.1. Creating a Bibliography Database

This section covers creating a .bib file that contains the bibliographic information you want to cite in your documents. You can use an ordinary text editor to create a bibliographic database (as described in Section 5.1.2) but it can be difficult to remember the names of the required fields and it's easy to make syntactic mistakes. It can also be hard to keep track of entries in a large database. To make life easier, there are a number of bibliography reference managers available that provide a convenient graphical interface. One such application is JabRef and is described next.

5.1.1. JabRef

I've chosen to describe JabRef here because it's an open source Java application that can run on any operating system that has the Java Runtime Environment[5.4] installed (at least version 1.5). You can download JabRef from http://jabref.sourceforge. net/download.php. Linux users may also be able to install it via their "Add/Remove Software" tool. (If you have successfully been using arara, you already have Java installed.)

Once you have installed it, run JabRef and select File→New database to create a new database (see Figure 5.1 on the next page). When you save your data, it's saved as a BibTeX (.bib) file.

Note that if you use the inputenc package in your thesis (see Volume 1 [15, §4.3.1]) you'll have to make sure JabRef is using the same encoding as your document. You can do this by selecting Options→Preferences to open the Preferences dialog box and set the default encoding as appropriate. For example, I use UTF-8 so I've set that as the default encoding (see Figure 5.2 on page 54). I also need to change the database encoding in the "Database properties" dialog, Figure 5.3 on page 54, which can be opened using File→Database properties.

To create a new entry you can select BibTeX→New entry, which will open the dialog box shown in Figure 5.4 on page 55. Now you need to click on the button appropriate to the entry. For example, click on "Article" for an article in a journal or click on "Inproceedings" for a paper in a conference proceedings.

EXAMPLE (BOOK):
Suppose I want to enter information about a book. I need to select BibTeX→New entry and then click on the button labelled "Book". This now displays fields in which I can enter the relevant information (see Figure 5.5 on page 56).

Next I need to enter information in the "Required fields" tab. This will usually include the title and the author. I also need to specify a key that uniquely identifies this entry. If you have read Volume 1 [15, §5.6] this key corresponds to the mandatory argument of \bibitem and is also used in \cite. Figure 5.6 on page 57 shows the details for my new entry. I've set the key to the author's surname followed by the year to make it easy to remember. This key won't appear anywhere in the document,

---

[5.4]http://www.java.com/getjava/

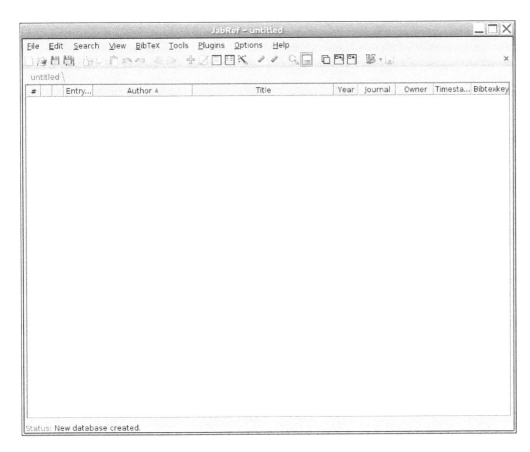

Figure 5.1. JabRef

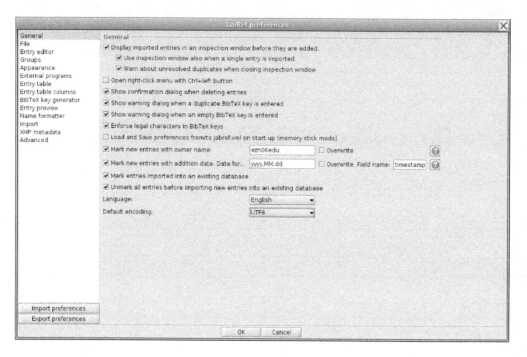

Figure 5.2. JabRef Preferences

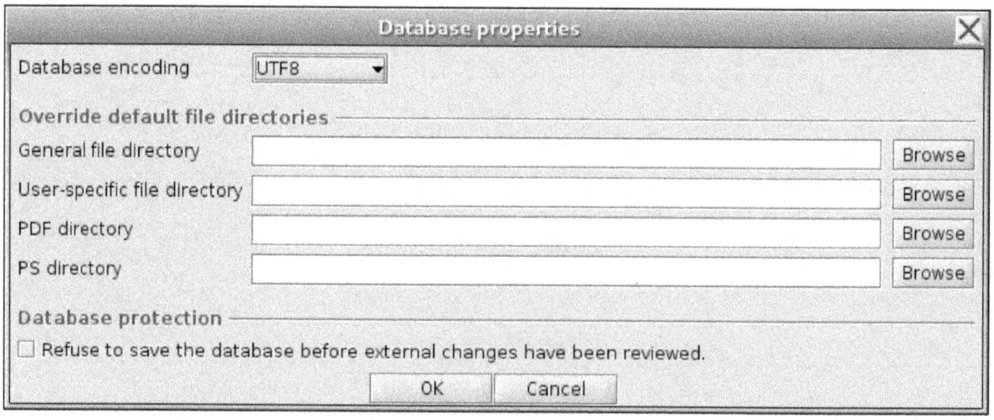

Figure 5.3. JabRef Database Properties

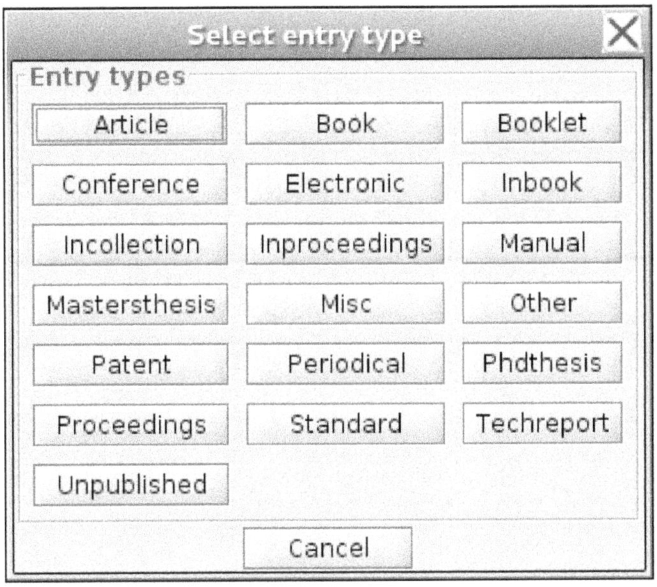

Figure 5.4. JabRef (Select Entry Type)

it's just used to identify the entry, just like the \label/\ref mechanism. Alternatively, I can click on the "Generate BibTeX Key" button ⚡ to automatically insert a unique key.

There are also optional fields you can specify as well. In Figure 5.7 on page 58, I've added the book's edition.

EXAMPLE (JOURNAL ARTICLE):

Now I want to enter an article in a journal. So I need to go back to BibTeX→New entry and click on "Article". This time I've used the "Generate BibTeX Key" button to generate the key to save me typing. (See Figure 5.8 on page 59.) I've also used the "General" tab to enter the DOI for this article. The entry now has an icon ⬛ next to it. I can click on this button to direct my web browser to the article's entry on the Internet.

BibTeX uses the European assumption that names are composed of forenames, an optional "von" part which starts with a lower case letter, a surname and an optional "jr" part. In order to enable BibTeX to correctly identify these components, names in the author or editor fields must be entered in one of the formats listed in Table 5.1 on the next page.

[FAQ: BibTeX sorting and name prefixes]

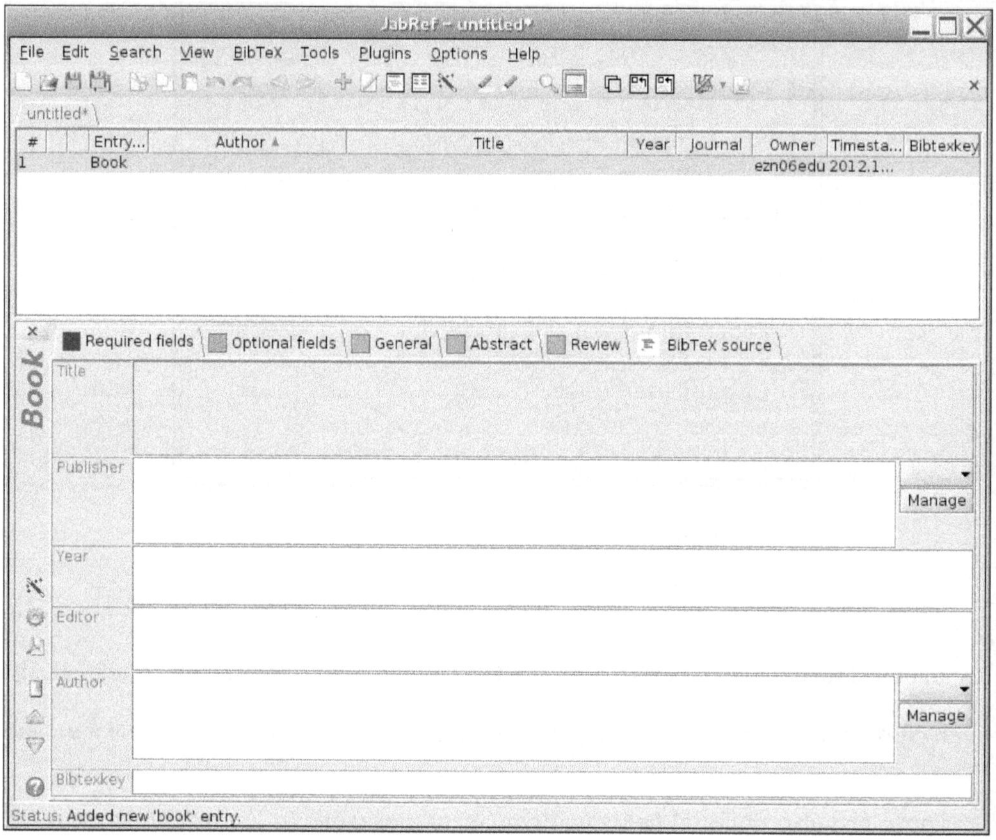

Figure 5.5. JabRef (New Entry)

Table 5.1. Name Formats for Bibliographic Data

⟨*forenames*⟩ ⟨*von*⟩ ⟨*surname*⟩
⟨*von*⟩ ⟨*surname*⟩, ⟨*forenames*⟩
⟨*von*⟩ ⟨*surname*⟩, ⟨*jr*⟩, ⟨*forenames*⟩

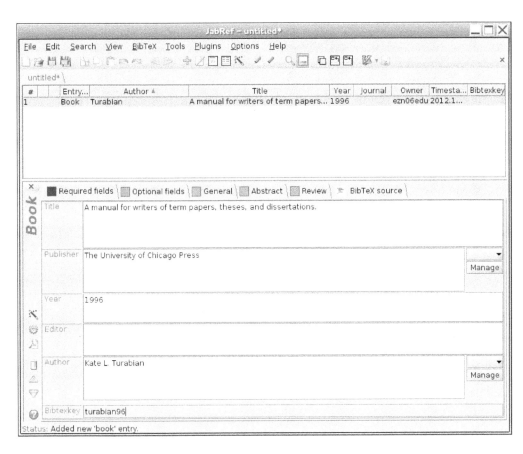

Figure 5.6. JabRef (Entering the Required Fields)

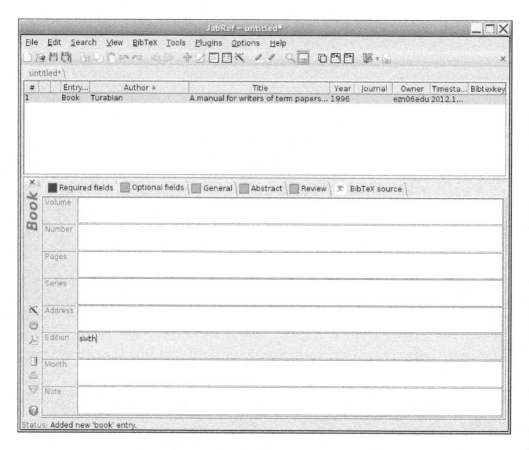

Figure 5.7. JabRef (Entering Optional Fields)

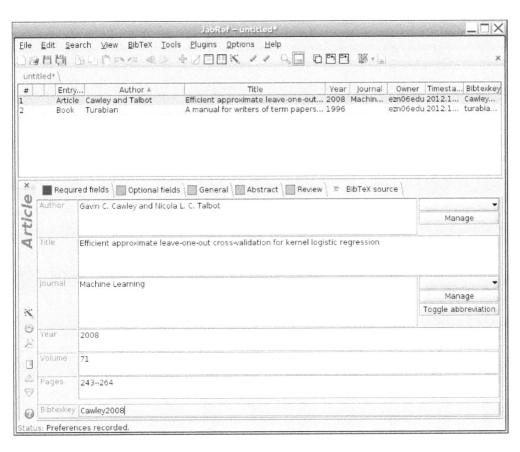

Figure 5.8. JabRef (Adding an Article)

EXAMPLES:

Entry	Abbreviated as
Alex Thomas von Neumann	A.T. von Neumann
John Chris {Smith Jones}	J.C. Smith Jones
van de Klee, Mary-Jane	M.-J. van de Klee
Smith, Jr, Fred John	F.J. Smith, Jr
Maria {\MakeUppercase{d}e La} Cruz	M. De La Cruz

Compare the last example with: Maria De La Cruz which would be abbreviated to: M. D. L. Cruz, which is incorrect. Let's analyse this last example in more detail: BibTeX always expects the "von" part to start with a lower case letter, but "De" and "La" both start with an upper case letter, so BibTeX will assume that these form part of the forenames. However, BibTeX will ignore any LaTeX commands such as \MakeUppercase in \MakeUppercase{d}e since it assumes that the command is an accent command. So when it parses \MakeUppercase{d}e it will skip \MakeUppercase and look at the following letter. In this case it is "d" which is lower case, so from BibTeX's point of view the word \MakeUppercase{d}e starts with a lower case letter ("d"), so it is therefore the "von" part. You can either do the same with the "La" part, or, as in the above example, you can place it in the same group as \MakeUppercase{d}e.

[FAQ: Case-changing oddities]

[FAQ: Accents in bibliographies]

Multiple authors should be separated by the keyword "and". **Don't use a comma to separate the authors.** Here is an example with three authors:

Input   Gavin C. Cawley and Nicola L. C. Talbot and Mark Girolami

If the author is an institution or company that happens to have the word "and" in its name, such as "Smith and Jones Inc", then you need to group the "and" to indicate that you mean the word "and" rather than the keyword:

Input   Smith {and} Jones Inc

Figure 5.9 on the facing page shows the entry for a paper in a conference proceedings, so for that one I used BibTeX→New entry and clicked on the "Inproceedings" button.

Notice the way I've written the title for this entry:

Input ↑
Input ↓

Sparse multinomial logistic regression via {Bayesian} {L1} regularisation

BibTeX automatically converts the title to lower case (apart from the initial letter) but here both "Bayesian" and "L1" should begin with a capital. I therefore need to enclose those words in braces to instruct BibTeX not to convert their case.

Multiple editors must also be separated by the "and" keyword, as shown in Figure 5.10 on page 62. For that entry, the editors are listed as:

Input   Bernhard Schölkopf and John Platt and Thomas Hofmann

Note that if I don't use the inputenc package, I need to change this to:

Input   Bernhard Sch\"{o}lkopf and John Platt and Thomas Hofmann

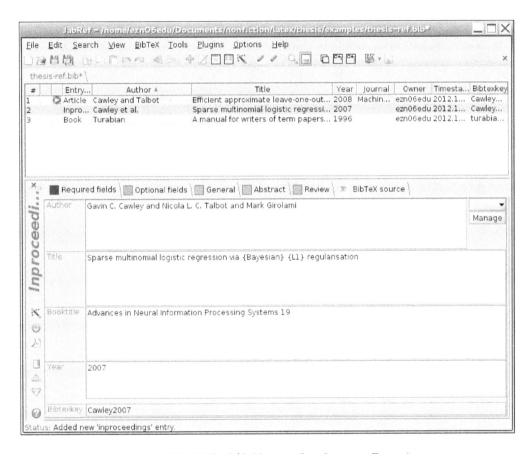

Figure 5.9. JabRef (Adding a Conference Paper)

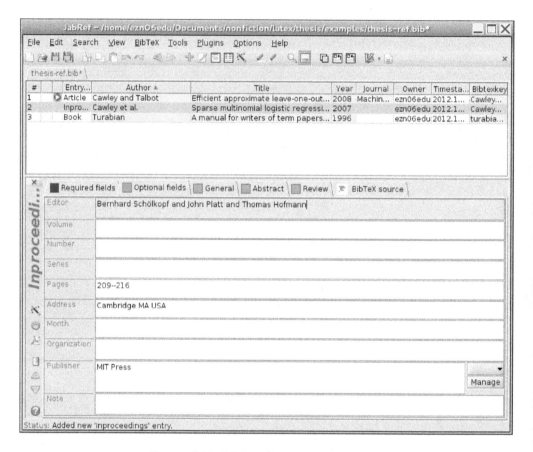

Figure 5.10. JabRef (Adding Editor List)

It's also possible to import entries from other formats, such as Copac or ISI, using File→Import into new database or file→Import into current database. Alternatively, you can copy and paste a plain text reference using BibTeX→New entry from plain text. This again opens the dialog box where you need to click on the entry type, but then it opens the "Plain text import" window.

EXAMPLE:
Suppose I want to add an entry for an article whose DOI is 10.1007/s10994-008-5055-9. First, I direct my browser to http://dx.doi.org/10.1007/s10994-008-5055-9, which takes me to the article's web page. In this case, it's in a journal published by Springer, so my browser is redirected to the SpringerLink cite. There I can use the export as text only option, then copy and paste the reference into JabRef's import window, as shown in Figure 5.11.

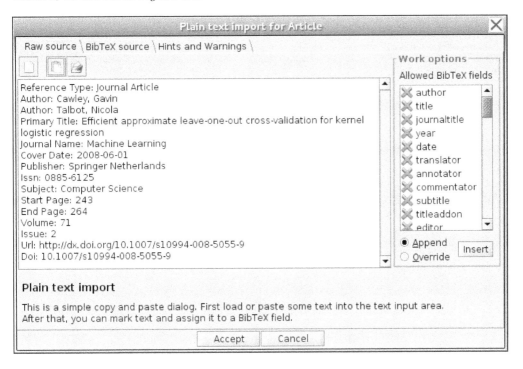

Figure 5.11. Importing a Plain Text Reference

Next, I need to select text, for example an author's name, and select the appropriate field in the "Work options" list. Then click on the "Insert" button. For example, in Figure 5.12 on the next page I have selected an author's name then I selected the "author" field in the "Work options" list.

Next I clicked on the "Insert" button. Now the author's name is highlighted in red and the author field has a tick next to it (see Figure 5.13 on page 65). I can repeat this process for the next author. (Just make sure the "Append" rather than "Override" radio button is selected.)

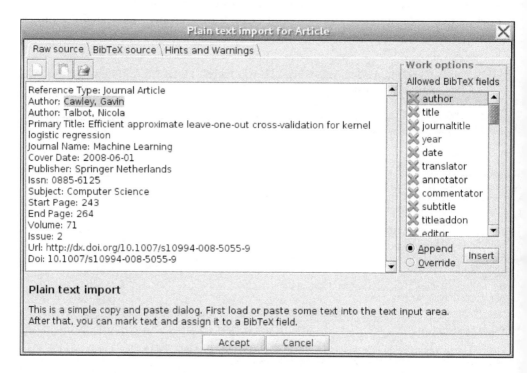

Figure 5.12. Importing a Plain Text Reference (Selecting a Field)

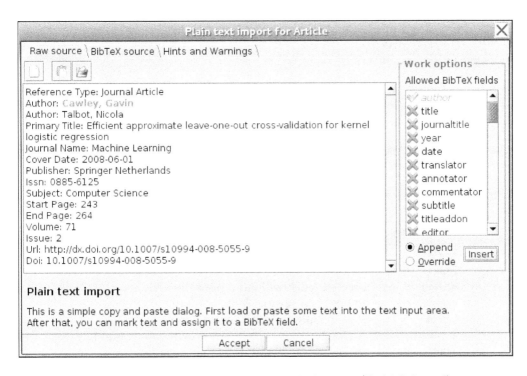

Figure 5.13. Importing a Plain Text Reference (Field Selected)

I can repeat this for all the different fields. Each time, I select the text in the raw source panel, then select the appropriate field from the "Work options" list and then click "Insert". Once I have finished, I then need to click "Accept".

5.1.2. Writing the .bib File Manually

It may be that you don't want to or can't use a bibliography management application, such as JabRef. In which case, you can create the .bib file in an ordinary text editor, such as the one you use to write your LaTeX documents. When you save the file, make sure you give it the extension .bib. Entries in this file should have the following form:

[FAQ: Creating a BibTeX bibliography]

@⟨*entry type*⟩{⟨*keyword*⟩,
    ⟨*field name*⟩ = "⟨*text*⟩",

$$\vdots$$

    ⟨*field name*⟩ = "⟨*text*⟩"
}

where ⟨*entry type*⟩ indicates the type of entry (e.g. book or article). Standard entry types are listed in Table 5.2.

Table 5.2. Standard BiBTeX entry types

Entry Name	Description
article	Article from a journal
book	Published book
booklet	Printed work without a publisher
conference	Identical to inproceedings
inbook	Part, chapter, section etc of a book
incollection	A chapter of a book with its own author and title
inproceedings	An article in a conference proceedings
manual	Technical documentation
mastersthesis	A master's thesis
misc	Non-standard work
phdthesis	PhD thesis
proceedings	Conference proceedings
techreport	Report published by an institution
unpublished	Unpublished work with an author and title

Within an entry, ⟨*keyword*⟩ is a short label that is used to cite this work with the \cite command. If you have written bibliographies with the thebibliography environment, it's the same as the argument to \bibitem. There then follows a comma-separated list of fields of the form ⟨*field name*⟩ = ⟨*value*⟩. The ⟨*field name*⟩ indicates what kind of field it is, e.g. title or author. Table 5.3 on the facing page lists the standard fields. Note that some bibliography styles may define additional non-standard fields, such as email or url. See the BibTEX documentation [11] for information about other fields not listed in Table 5.3.

[FAQ: URLS in BibTeX bibliographies]

Table 5.3. Standard BiBTeX fields

address	Publisher/Institution's address
author	Author names
booktitle	Title of book where only a part of the book is being cited
chapter	Chapter or section number
edition	The edition of the book
howpublished	How a non-standard work was published
institution	The institute sponsoring the work
journal	The name of the journal
month	The month the work was published
note	Any additional information
number	The number of the journal, technical report etc
organization	Organization sponsoring conference or manual
pages	Page number or page range
publisher	Publisher's name
school	Academic institution where thesis was written
series	Name of a series
title	The title of the work
type	The type of technical report
volume	The volume number.

The required and optional fields for the standard entry types are listed in Table 5.4 on the following page. If an entry has a field that is neither required nor optional, BibTeX will ignore it. This means that you can have a field called, say, abstract, which will be ignored by the standard bibliography styles, but will be included if you use a bibliography style that has an abstract field. So you can store additional information in the database that won't appear in the bibliography.

The author and editor fields have the same format as described in Section 5.1.1. That is, each name should be in one of the forms listed in Table 5.1 on page 56, and multiple authors or editors must be separated with the keyword "and".

EXAMPLE (MULTIPLE AUTHORS):
This example uses the book entry:

↑ Input

```
@book{goossens97,
    author = "Goossens, Michel and Rahtz, Sebastian and
            Mittelbach, Frank",
    title = "The \LaTeX\ graphics companion: illustrating
            documents with \TeX\ and {PostScript}",
    publisher = "Addison Wesley Longman, Inc",
```

Table 5.4. Required and Optional Fields

Entry Type	Required Fields	Optional Fields
article	author, title, journal, year	volume, month, note, number, pages
book	author or editor, title, publisher, year	address, edition, volume or number, month, note, pages, series
booklet	title	author, address, howpublished, month, note, year
inbook	author or editor, chapter or pages, title, publisher, year	address, edition, volume or number, month, note, series, type
incollection	author, title, booktitle, publisher, year	address, chapter, editor, edition, volume or number, month, note, pages, series, type
inproceedings	author, title, booktitle, year	address, editor, volume or number, month, note, organization, pages, publisher, series, type
manual	title	author, address, edition, month, note, organization, year
mastersthesis	author, title, school, year	address, month, note, type
misc	—	author, howpublished, month, note, title, year
phdthesis	author, title, school, year	address, month, note, type
proceedings	title, year	editor, organization, address, volume or number, series, month, publisher, note
techreport	author, title, institution, year	type, number, address, month, note
unpublished	author, title, note	month, year

```
    year = 1997
}
```
↓ Input

In this example, the ⟨keyword⟩ is goossens97. That is the identifying key used in \cite, described below. The standard bibliography styles usually convert titles to lower case, so the name PostScript is enclosed in curly braces to prevent this from happening.

Note that curly braces {} can be used instead of double quotes. The above example can just as easily be written:

↑ Input

```
@book{goossens97,
    author = {Goossens, Michel and Rahtz, Sebastian and
              Mittelbach, Frank},
    title = {The \LaTeX\ graphics companion: illustrating
             documents with \TeX\ and {PostScript}},
    publisher = {Addison Wesley Longman, Inc},
    year = 1997
}
```
↓ Input

Numbers (such as the year 1997) don't need to be delimited with quotes or braces. So you can have

```
pages = 10
```
Input

but a page range would need to be delimited:

```
pages = "10--45"
```
Input

Bibliography styles always have three-letter abbreviations for months: jan, feb, mar, etc. These should be used instead of typing them in explicitly, as their format depends on the bibliography style. These abbreviations should be entered without quotes. For example:

↑ Input

```
@inproceedings{talbot97,
    author    = "Talbot, Nicola and Cawley, Gavin",
    title     = "A fast index assignment algorithm for
                 robust vector quantisation of image data",
    booktitle = "Proceedings of the I.E.E.E. International
                 Conference on Image Processing",
    address   = "Santa Barbara, California, USA",
    month     = oct,
    year      = 1997
}
```
↓ Input

5.2. BibTeX

Now that we've created a .bib file (as described above) we next need to look at how to incorporate the information in the database into a LaTeX document. As mentioned in Volume 1 [15, §5.6], entries are cited in the document using:

Definition \cite[⟨*text*⟩]{⟨*key list*⟩}

where ⟨*key list*⟩ is a comma-separated list of keys. Each key uniquely identifies an entry in the database. If you used JabRef (Section 5.1.1), this is the key you entered in the "Bibtexkey" field. If you wrote the .bib file in a text editor (Section 5.1.2) it's the ⟨*keyword*⟩ bit at the start of the list of fields for the entry.

[FAQ: Choosing a bibliography style]
Next you need to specify what type of bibliography style you want to use. There are many available, but the basic ones are:

abbrv Entries sorted alphabetically with abbreviated first names, months and journal names.

alpha Entries sorted alphabetically with the citation represented by abbreviated author surname and year instead of a number.

plain Entries sorted alphabetically, with the citation represented by a number.

unsrt Entries sorted according to citation with the citation represented by a number.

The style is specified in your LaTeX document with the command:

Definition \bibliographystyle{⟨*style*⟩}

where ⟨*style*⟩ is the name of the style. Some people put this command in the document's preamble and some people put it near their bibliography, but wherever you choose to put it, this command should only be used once.

The actual bibliography itself is input into the document using

Definition \bibliography{⟨*database*⟩}

where ⟨*database*⟩ is the name of the database *without the .bib extension*. In fact, this argument can be a comma-separated list of databases if your entries are stored across multiple files.

Recall the example thesis in Listing 1 on page 16 ended with:

Input ↑
```
% The bibliography will go here

\end{document}
```
Input ↓

If my references are stored in the file `thesis-ref.bib`[5.5], then I can replace the above comment as follows:

Listing 15[5.6]

↑ Input

```
\bibliographystyle{plain}
\bibliography{thesis-ref}

\end{document}
```

↓ Input

Elsewhere in my document I need some citations. For example:

↑ Input

```
See Turabian~\cite{turabian96} for a comprehensive guide on preparing
a thesis.
```

↓ Input

If you are using arara (see Section 1.1.2) you need the following lines in your source code:

↑ Input

```
% arara: pdflatex: { synctex: on }
% arara: bibtex
% arara: pdflatex: { synctex: on }
% arara: pdflatex: { synctex: on }
```

↓ Input

If you are using `latexmk` (see Section 1.1.1) make sure you are using the `-bibtex` argument (Figure 1.5 on page 7).

If you are not using either `latexmk` or arara, you will need to run PDFLATEX, then run BibTEX, then run PDFLATEX twice more (see Section 1.1).

If your citations appear as two question marks ?? in your PDF, then the citation key you used hasn't been recognised. This could be that you've forgotten the BibTEX and subsequent *two* PDFLATEX calls, or it could be that the key hasn't been defined, or you have misspelt it.

Recall from Volume 1 [15, §5.6] that the bibliography doesn't usually get added to the table of contents for most class files, but the KOMA-Script classes provide the options bibliography=totocnumbered and bibliography=totoc, that add a numbered or unnumbered bibliography to the table of contents.

You can add backlinks from your bibliography back to the section or page where the entries were cited using the `backref` option of the hyperref package. (The hyperref package should usually be loaded last.) For example, to have backreferences to the pages on which the citation occurs:

```
\usepackage[backref]{hyperref}
```

Input

The hyperref package is covered in more detail in Volume 4 [14].

[5.5]http://www.dickimaw-books.com/latex/thesis/html/examples/thesis-ref.bib
[5.6]http://www.dickimaw-books.com/latex/thesis/html/examples/thesis-biblio.tex

5.2.1. Author–Year Citations

The default behaviour of citations with bibliography styles such as `plain` is to produce a numerical reference in square brackets. If you're using `bibtex` (rather than biblatex, described below) you can override this using a number of packages. One such package is natbib. This comes with some drop-in replacements for the standard bibliography styles: plainnat, unsrtnat and abbrvnat. The natbib package comes with a variety of package options, but I'm just going to mention a few of them: authoryear for author–year citations (default), numbers for numerical citations, super for superscripted numerical citations, round for round parentheses, square for square parentheses and sort&compress which sorts multiple citations and compresses consecutive numbers into a range. For example, [4,2,8,3] will become [2–4,8].

So for citations that give the author and year rather than a number, you need to load natbib in the preamble:

Input   `\usepackage[round]{natbib}`

and specify one of the natbib bibliography styles:

Input   `\bibliographystyle{plainnat}`

There are two main replacements for `\cite`:

Definition   `\citet[⟨pre⟩][⟨post⟩]{⟨key⟩}`

for textual citations and

Definition   `\citep[⟨pre⟩][⟨post⟩]{⟨key⟩}`

for parenthetical citations.

Unlike `\cite`, these commands have two optional arguments. The second ⟨post⟩ is a suffix, the same as `\cite`'s only optional argument. The first optional argument ⟨pre⟩ is a prefix. If only one optional argument is present, it is assumed to be ⟨post⟩, so if you only want a prefix and no suffix, you have to specify an empty argument for ⟨post⟩.

EXAMPLE:
(Using the same `thesis-ref.bib`[5.7] database as earlier.)

Input ↑

> Listing 16[5.8]

A textual citation `\citet{turabian96}` and a parenthetical citation

Input ↓   `\citep[see][Chapter 9]{goossens97}`.

Result:

[5.7]http://www.dickimaw-books.com/latex/thesis/html/examples/thesis-ref.bib
[5.8]http://www.dickimaw-books.com/latex/thesis/html/examples/thesis-nat.tex

A textual citation Turabian (1996) and a parenthetical citation (see Goossens et al., 1997, Chapter 9).

↑ Output

↓ Output

5.2.2. Troubleshooting

- BibTeX writes the thebibliography environment to a .bbl file, which is then input into the document by \bibliography. If you have made a LaTeX error in the .bib file, this error will be copied to the .bbl file. If you have corrected the error in the .bib file, but you are still getting an error when you LaTeX your document, try deleting the .bbl file. (In TeXworks, you can use the menu item File→Remove Aux Files.)

- Remember to use double quotes or braces to delimit the field names in your .bib file.

- Remember to put a comma at the end of each field entry (except the last).

- It is better to only use alphanumerical characters in the keywords. Some punctuation characters such as . (full stop) should be fine (unless you're using a package such as babel that makes them active), but spaces are not recommended, and commas should definitely be avoided.

- If you have entered a field in the .bib file, but it doesn't appear in the bibliography, check to make sure that the field is required or optional for that type of entry, and check the spelling. (You can avoid this problem by using a bibliography management system such as JabRef.)

- Check the BibTeX log file (.blg) for messages.

- If you get an error that looks something like:

```
ERROR - Cannot find control file 'thesis-ref.bcf'! - did you pass
the "backend=biber" option to BibLaTeX?
```

then you have inadvertently used biber (see below) instead of bibtex.

- If you get an error that looks something like:

```
I found no \citation commands---while reading file thesis1.aux
I found no \bibdata command---while reading file thesis1.aux
I found no \bibstyle command---while reading file thesis1.aux
```

then you probably forgot to use the \bibliography and \bibliographystyle commands in your document.

5.3. Biblatex

The biblatex package is a reimplementation of LaTeX's bibliographic facilities. The formatting of the bibliography is governed by LaTeX commands instead of selecting a BibTeX style (as was done with \bibliographystyle described above). This package uses biber[5.9] instead of BibTeX to process the bibliographic database and sort the entries. Legacy BibTeX is also supported, but with a reduced feature set. The biblatex package also supports multiple bibliographies, for example a bibliography for each chapter in the document. The biblatex package requires e-TeX, so make sure you have a recent TeX distribution. Biber comes with the latest version of TeX Live.

If you are using JabRef (described in Section 5.1.1) there is a BibLaTeX mode option in the Advanced tab of the JabRef preferences dialog, illustrated in Figure 5.14. (Use Options→Preferences to open the dialog.) You will have to quit and restart JabRef after enabling this option. When you restart, you should find extra fields when you edit an entry or create a new entry, as illustrated in Figure 5.15 on the next page. You should also find that there are more entry types available (see Figure 5.16 on page 76).

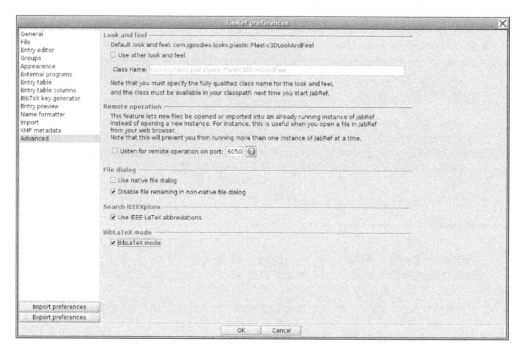

Figure 5.14. JabRef Advanced Preferences

With BibTeX, there was a month and year field. BibLaTeX provides a replacement date field, although if this field is missing it will fall back on the month and year fields. In Figure 5.17 on page 77, I've edited my earlier example to use the new date field.

[5.9]http://biblatex-biber.sourceforge.net/

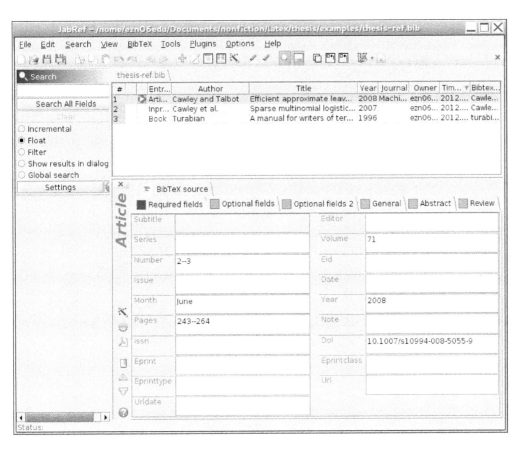

Figure 5.15. JabRef in BibLaTeX Mode

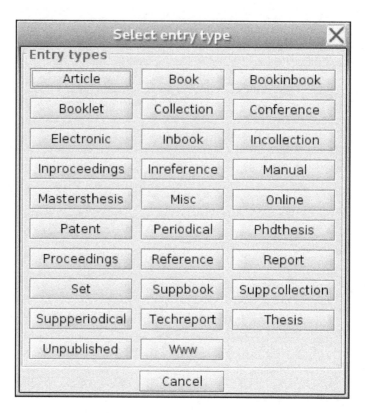

Figure 5.16. JabRef in BibLaTeX Mode (Select Entry Type)

Note that the date should be specified as ⟨*year*⟩-⟨*month*⟩-⟨*day*⟩ where -⟨*day*⟩ or -⟨*month*⟩-⟨*day*⟩ maybe omitted. A slash / should be used to indicate a range, for example `2002-01/2002-02`.

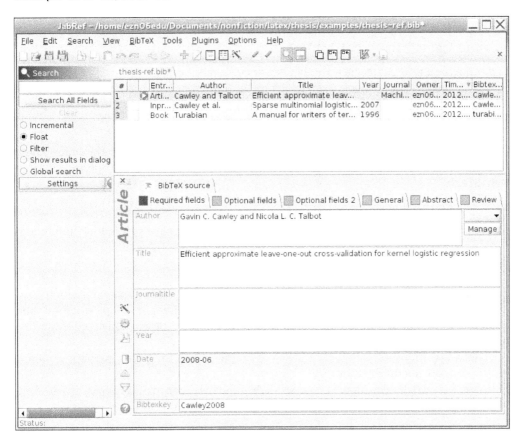

Figure 5.17. JabRef in BibLaTeX Mode (Setting the Publication Date)

Recall from Figure 5.2 on page 54 and Figure 5.3 on page 54 that I set the default encoding to UTF-8. With BibLaTeX and `biber`, my UTF-8 bibliography can be correctly sorted, but I need to make sure that I load the inputenc package before biblatex in my document:

```
\usepackage[utf8]{inputenc}
\usepackage{biblatex}
```
Input
Input

Section 5.2.1 described the natbib package. BibLaTeX has a compatibility module:

```
\usepackage[natbib]{biblatex}
```
Input

This provides the same commands (such as `\citet` and `\citep`) that natbib provides.

The default sorting order is name, title and year. This can be changed using the sorting package option. For example, to sort by name, year and title:

Input   `\usepackage[sorting=nyt]{biblatex}`

Or you can suppress the sorting, so that all entries are in citation order:

Input   `\usepackage[sorting=none]{biblatex}`

For other possible values, see the biblatex documentation [9].

If you want a list of back-references in the bibliography, referring to the pages on which the entries were cited, you can use the `backref` option:

Input   `\usepackage[backref]{biblatex}`

The default database backend is biber, which is recommended, but if for some reason you want to stick to using bibtex you can use the backend option to switch to bibtex:

Input   `\usepackage[backend=bibtex]{biblatex}`

There are also options that govern whether certain fields are printed in the bibliography, such as isbn, url or doi. For example:

Input   `\usepackage[isbn,url,doi]{biblatex}`

The style can be set using the `style` option. The default is numeric, which produces a numeric citation, such as [1]. There is also numeric-comp, which is like natbib's sort&compress option, described in Section 5.2.1, or authoryear which displays ⟨author⟩ ⟨year⟩ citations.

There are many other citation styles. For these and for other package options, see the biblatex documentation [9].

With BibLaTeX, you don't use the \bibliography command, described in Section 5.2. Instead, you add the bib file as a resource *in the preamble* using:

Definition   `\addbibresource[⟨options⟩]{⟨resource⟩}`

where ⟨resource⟩ is the name of the bib file *including the file extension*. However, the resource doesn't have to be a bib file. You can only add one resource at a time:

Input ↑   `\addbibresource{bibfile1.bib}`
Input ↓   `\addbibresource{bibfile2.bib}`

The resource can be a remote one, in which case you need to use the location option with the value remote and specify the URL:

Input ↑
Input ↓   `\addbibresource[location=remote]{http://www.somewhere.com/bibfile2.bib}`

This is only available if you use biber as the backend. Another option is datatype which specifies the format of the resource. The default is bibtex, but it can also be `ris`, `zoterordfxm` or `endnotexml`. See the biblatex and biber documentation [7] for further details.

The bibliography itself is displayed using

`\printbibliography[⟨options⟩]` Definition

This should go in the document where you want the bibliography to be displayed.

Like the natbib commands described in Section 5.2.1, the biblatex commands generally have two optional arguments, indicating the prenote and postnote, and a mandatory argument specifying the key or a comma-separated list of keys. If you want a prenote but not a postnote, you need to give an empty second optional argument. The basic commands are:

`\cite[⟨prenote⟩][⟨postnote⟩]{⟨key⟩}`
`\Cite[⟨prenote⟩][⟨postnote⟩]{⟨key⟩}` Definition

These are bare citation commands. The latter is provided if the citation occurs at the start of a sentence.

`\parencite[⟨prenote⟩][⟨postnote⟩]{⟨key⟩}`
`\Parencite[⟨prenote⟩][⟨postnote⟩]{⟨key⟩}` Definition

These commands are like `\cite` and `\Cite` but enclose the citation in parentheses (square if the numeric style is used).

`\textcite[⟨prenote⟩][⟨postnote⟩]{⟨key⟩}`
`\Textcite[⟨prenote⟩][⟨postnote⟩]{⟨key⟩}` Definition

These commands are used for citations in the flow of text. The latter is provided if the citation occurs at the start of a sentence. For other citation commands, see the biblatex documentation [9].

So, the example document from Listing 1 on page 16, can now be edited so that the preamble looks like:

Listing 17[5.10]

⊤ Input

```
% arara: pdflatex: { synctex: on }
% arara: biber
% arara: pdflatex: { synctex: on }
% arara: pdflatex: { synctex: on }
\documentclass[oneside]{scrbook}

\usepackage[backend=biber]{biblatex}

\addbibresource{thesis-refs.bib}
```

↓ Input

[5.10]`http://www.dickimaw-books.com/latex/thesis/html/examples/thesis-biblatex.tex`

(where `thesis-refs.bib`[5.11] is the name of my bibliography database, see Section 5.1) and the end of the document looks like:

Input ↑

```
\printbibliography

\end{document}
```

Input ↓

Elsewhere in the document, I need to cite some of the entries in my bibliography database:

Input ↑

```
First of all, let's cite a book~\parencite{wainwright93} now let's cite
a journal paper and a conference
proceedings~\parencite{cawley96,talbot97}. Finally, let's cite a chapter
in a book~\parencite[Chapter 9]{goossens97}.
```

Input ↓

If you want to build the document using arara (Section 1.1.2) remember to include the % arara: comments (as shown above). If you are using `latexmk` (Section 1.1.1) remember to use the -bibtex option as illustrated in Figure 1.5 on page 7.

If you're not using an automated method, such as arara or `latexmk`, you need a PDFLaTeX run, a biber run (or bibtex if you've chosen that as your backend) followed by two more PDFLaTeX runs.

5.3.1. Troubleshooting

Most of the comments from the BibTeX troubleshooting section (see page 73) also apply here. If you get an error that looks like:

```
I found no \citation commands---while reading file thesis-biblatex.aux
I found no \bibdata command---while reading file thesis-biblatex.aux
I found no \bibstyle command---while reading file thesis-biblatex.aux
```

then you have inadvertently used bibtex instead of biber. If you actually want to use bibtex with the biblatex package remember that you have to specify bibtex using:

Input

```
\usepackage[backend=bibtex]{biblatex}
```

[5.11]`http://www.dickimaw-books.com/latex/thesis/html/examples/thesis-refs.bib`

CHAPTER 6

GENERATING INDEXES AND GLOSSARIES

Most theses will need a glossary of terms or a list of acronyms or notation. It's less likely that you'll need an index in your thesis, but since the same mechanism is used to generate glossaries and indexes, both topics are covered in this chapter. There are two basic methods of generating a glossary or index:

1. The glossary or indexing information is written to a temporary file by LaTeX while the document is being built. An external application is then used to collate and sort the entries defined in that temporary file and LaTeX code to display the result is written to another file. You then need to run (PDF)LaTeX on your document to ensure the sorted and collated glossary or index is displayed. (You may then need an additional LaTeX run to ensure the table of contents is up-to-date.) This is similar to the way you had to use `bibtex` or `biber` between LaTeX runs in the previous chapter.

2. The glossary or indexing information is collated and sorted by LaTeX during the document build. (At least two runs are required, but no external indexing application is needed.)

The first approach (see Section 6.1) is more efficient, but a lot of users, especially beginners, have difficulty with the intermediate step where the external indexing application is run. The second approach (see Section 6.2) is slower, but you don't need to worry about running an indexing application. If you're not writing in English (in particular if you are not using the Latin alphabet) you're better off using the first approach with `xindy`. In this chapter I'll describe both approaches and you can choose which you prefer.

6.1. Using an External Indexing Application

This section describes how to create indexes (Section 6.1.1) or glossaries (Section 6.1.2) using an external indexing application. There are two popular indexing applications: `makeindex` and `xindy`. All TeX distributions should come with `makeindex`. The TeX Live distribution also comes with `xindy`, but if you have a different TeX distribution (such as MikTeX) you may need to fetch `xindy` from `http://www.xindy.org/`.

NOTE:
You must have Perl installed in order to use `xindy` as it's a Perl script. (See §2.20 from Volume 1.) If you have successfully been using `latexmk`, you already have Perl installed.

6.1.1. Creating an Index (makeidx package)

Volume 1 [15, §8] introduced the command:

Definition   `\index{⟨text⟩}`

to index the word given in ⟨*text*⟩. For example, if `\index{circuit}` occurs on page 42, then "42" will be added to the *location list* for the term "circuit".

NOTE:
`\index` doesn't display any text. It just adds a line to the index file with the information required by `makeindex` or `xindy` to sort and collate the information.

The default action of `\index` simply ignores its argument. To ensure the indexing mechanism works, you must activate it by placing

Definition   `\makeindex`

in the document preamble.

Finally, you need to use

Definition   `\printindex`

(defined in the makeidx package) to display the index.

NOTE:
`\printindex` won't produce any text until you have run the external indexing application.

Here's an example document:

Input ↑   ┌─ Listing 18[6.1]

```
% arara: pdflatex: { synctex: on }
% arara: makeindex
% arara: pdflatex: { synctex: on }
\documentclass[12pt,oneside]{scrbook}

\usepackage{makeidx}

\makeindex

\title{Sample Document}
```

―――――――――――――――――――――――
[6.1]`http://www.dickimaw-books.com/latex/thesis/html/examples/sample-index.tex`

```
\author{Me}

\begin{document}
\maketitle

\chapter{Sample}

Stuff about eigenvectors\index{eigenvector} and
eigenvalues\index{eigenvalue}.

\chapter{Another Sample}

Some more stuff about eigenvectors\index{eigenvector} and
eigenvalues\index{eigenvalue}. Something about
eigen-decomposition\index{eigen-decomposition}.

\backmatter

\printindex

\end{document}
```

↓ Input

If you are using arara to build your document (see Section 1.1.2), remember to include the % arara: comments, as shown in the above listing. If you are using latexmk to build your document, remember to include the .idx custom dependency to your RC file, as described in Section 1.1.1.

If you aren't using an automated method to build your document, you will need to run PDFLATEX, then run makeindex, and then run PDFLATEX again (see Section 1.1).

If you prefer to use xindy instead of makeindex, you need to run texindy (a xindy wrapper customised for LATEX documents). If you are using arara, change the line:

```
% arara: makeindex
```

to (change the language as required):

```
% arara: texindy: { language: english }
```

(Make sure you have added the texindy rule as described in Section 1.1.2.) If you are using latexmk to build your document, you will need to change the custom dependency for .idx files, as described in Section 1.1.1.

Overriding the Default Sort

By default the index entry will be sorted according to the word being indexed. However, you can override this by writing the argument of \index in the form:

⟨*sort*⟩@⟨*word*⟩

Definition

where ⟨*sort*⟩ is how to sort the term and ⟨*word*⟩ is how the term should appear in the index.

The `makeindex` application doesn't understand LaTeX commands. It simply sorts the term as is. So, for example, if you do

Input   `\index{\AE olian}`

then `makeindex` will sort it according to the characters \, A, E, ␣ (space), o, l, i, a, n. Since `makeindex` sorts symbols (such as \) before letters, it will put `\AE␣olian` before, say, adze, since \ comes before "a".

To get around this, you need to specify the sort key:

Input   `\index{AEolian@\AE olian}`

Now `makeindex` will put "Æolian" after "adze". Here's another example that indexes a function or method:

Input   `\index{sqrt()@\texttt{sqrt()}}`

You will also need to do something similar if you are entering the character directly via the inputenc package:

Input   `\index{elite@élite}`

Note, however, that you don't need to do this if you are using `xindy`. You just need to make sure you match the input encoding. For example:

Input ↑

```
% arara: pdflatex: { synctex: on }
% arara: texindy: { language: english, codepage: latin1}
% arara: pdflatex: { synctex: on }
\documentclass[12pt,oneside]{scrbook}

\usepackage[latin1]{inputenc}
\usepackage{makeidx}
```

Input ↓

Later in the document:

Input   `\index{élite}`

Setting the Location Format

Each index entry has an associated *location list* that directs the reader to the pages in the document associated with that entry. For example, if you look up `\index` in this book's index, the entry's location list will include this page. If the location list is long, it's helpful to highlight a particular location to direct the reader to the principle definition or discussion related to that term. This is usually done by formatting the relevant location in a different font, for example bold or italic.

You can specify the format for the location by writing the argument of \index in the form:

⟨*word*⟩|⟨*format*⟩   Definition

where ⟨*format*⟩ is the name of a text-block command *without* the leading backslash. For example:

`\index{eigenvector|textbf}`   Input

You can combine @ and |. For example:

`\index{sqrt()@\texttt{sqrt()}|textbf}`   Input

NOTE:
Make sure the format you use is the name of a command that takes an argument.
While it won't cause an error to use, say, `bfseries` instead of `textbf`, it will cause
the unexpected side-effect of rendering the rest of your index in that font, instead of
just that particular location.

You can also use ⟨*format*⟩ to cross-reference another entry. If you have an entry
that's just a synonym for another entry, you can use:

⟨*word*⟩|see{⟨*name*⟩}   Definition

where ⟨*name*⟩ is the other entry. If you want to direct the reader to a similar topic,
you can use:

⟨*word*⟩|seealso{⟨*topic*⟩}   Definition

where ⟨*topic*⟩ is the other entry.
For example:

`\index{eigenvector|seealso{eigenvalue}}`   Input

Sub Levels

An entry in the index may have sub-items. With `makeindex` you can have a maximum
of three levels. With `xindy` you can have an arbitrary number of levels. However,
it's a good idea to consider the advice in the Oxford Style Manual [12]: "In all but
the most complex indexes, subentries within subentries (*sub-subentries*) should be
avoided." In other words, just because it's possible to do something doesn't mean
you should do it.

To indicate a subentry, the argument of \index should be in the form:

⟨*main entry*⟩!⟨*subentry*⟩   Definition

For example:

`\index{reptile!caiman}`   Input

If you really must have a sub-subentry:

Input   \index{reptile!crocodylian!caiman}

You can combine @, | and !. For example:

Input   \index{methods!sqrt()@\texttt{sqrt()}|textbf}

Listing 17 on page 79 can now be modified as follows (download the document for the complete code):

Input ⊤̄   ┌─| Listing 19[6.2] |───

```
% In the preamble:
% arara: pdflatex: { synctex: on }
% arara: biber
% arara: makeindex
% arara: pdflatex: { synctex: on }
% arara: pdflatex: { synctex: on }
\documentclass[oneside,12pt]{scrbook}

\usepackage{makeidx}
\makeindex

% Later in the document:

Some sample code is shown in Listing~\ref{lst:sample}.
This uses the function \lstinline"sqrt()"%
\index{sqrt()@\texttt{sqrt()}}%
\index{functions!sqrt()@\texttt{sqrt()}}%
\index{square root|see{\texttt{sqrt()}}}.

\begin{Definition}[Tautology]
A \emph{tautology}\index{tautology|textbf} is a proposition
that is always true for any value of its variables.
\end{Definition}

\begin{Definition}[Contradiction]
A \emph{contradiction}\index{contradiction|textbf} is
a proposition that is always false for any
value of its variables.
\end{Definition}

% At the end of the document:

\printbibliography
```

───

[6.2] http://www.dickimaw-books.com/latex/thesis/html/examples/thesis-index.tex

```
\printindex

\end{document}
```

↓ Input

The index for the above document looks like:

↑ Output

contradiction, **2**

functions
    sqrt(), 2

sqrt(), 2
square root,
    see sqrt()

tautology, **2**

↓ Output

Troubleshooting

- My index hasn't appeared.

    1. Make sure you have the command \printindex at the place where you want the index to appear (this command is defined in the makeidx package).

    2. Make sure you have the command \makeindex in the preamble.

    3. If you are building the document using arara make sure you included all the % arara: directives as shown in Listing 19 on the preceding page. If you are using latexmk, make sure you have included the .idx dependency, as described in Section 1.1.1. If you're not using an automated tool, make sure you run (PDF)LATEX, then makeindex and then (PDF)LATEX again (see Section 1.1).

    4. Check makeindex's log file (which has the extension .ilg by default) for error messages.

- I want to index the character ", @, ! or | but it's not working.

    If you want any of these symbols in your index, you will need to prefix the character with the double-quote symbol ". For example to index the @ symbol:

    ```
    \index{"@}
    ```

    Input

- I have multiple entries of the same item. For example:

  identity matrix, 10, 22–30
  identity matrix, 4

  Check to make sure the sort argument to each of the corresponding \index commands is the same. Pay particular attention to spaces as makeindex will treat the following entries differently:

Input ↑

```
\index{identity␣matrix}
\index{identity␣␣matrix}
```

Input ↓

  LaTeX however treats multiple spaces the same as a single space, so the text will appear the same in the index.

- LaTeX says that the command \printindex is undefined.

  You have forgotten to load the makeidx package.

6.1.2. Creating Glossaries, Lists of Symbols or Acronyms (glossaries package)

There are a number of packages available to assist producing a list of acronyms (such as the acronym package) or a glossary (such as the nomencl package). You can see a list of available packages in the OnLine TeX Catalogue's Topic Index[6.3] [3]. Here, I've chosen to describe the glossaries package. Firstly, it encompasses the functionality of both acronym and nomencl as glossaries allows you to define multiple lists of acronyms, lists of symbols or glossaries. Secondly, I wrote the glossaries package, so it's the one with which I am most familiar.

The glossaries package is very flexible, but the downside to that is that it has too many features to cover briefly. I'm therefore only going to introduce the basics here. If you want more detail you'll have to read the user manual [16]. I will use the term "glossary" to mean a list of terms or a list of notation or a list of symbols or a list of acronyms.

NOTE:

If you want to use both glossaries and hyperref, you must load hyperref *before* glossaries. This is an exception to the usual advice of loading hyperref last.

[6.3]http://mirror.ctan.org/help/Catalogue/bytopic.html#index

Defining Glossary Entries

Firstly, in order to make the glossary (or glossaries, if you have more than one) appear, you must use the command

`\makeglossaries`   Definition

in the preamble. This is analogous to the `\makeindex` command described in Section 6.1.1.

Next you need to define the terms you want to appear in the glossary. This is done using the command:

`\newglossaryentry{⟨label⟩}{⟨key-val list⟩}`   Definition

The first argument ⟨*label*⟩ is a unique label so that you can refer to this entry in your document text. The entry will only appear in the glossary if you have referenced it in the document using one of the commands listed later. The second argument is a comma-separated list of ⟨*key*⟩=⟨*value*⟩ options. Common keys are:

- `name`

  The name of the entry (as it will appear in the glossary).

- `description`

  A brief description of this entry (to appear in the glossary).

- `text`

  How this entry will appear in the document text where the singular form is required. If this key is omitted the value of `name` will be used.

- `first`

  How this entry will appear in the document text the first time it is used, where the first use requires the singular form. If this key is omitted the value of `text` is used.

- `plural`

  How this entry will appear in the document text where the plural form is required. If this key is omitted, the value is obtained by appending the letter "s" to the value of the `text` key.

- `firstplural`

  How this entry will appear in the document text the first time it is used, where the first use requires the plural form. If this field is omitted, the value is obtained by appending the letter "s" to the value of the `first` key.

- `symbol`

  This key is provided to allow the user to specify an associated symbol, but most glossary styles ignore this value.

- sort

  This value indicates how to sort this entry (analogous to using the @ character in the argument of \index, as described in Section 6.1.1). If this key is omitted the value of name is used.

- type

  This is the glossary type to which this entry belongs (see Section 6.1.2). If omitted the main (default) glossary is assumed.

EXAMPLES:

The following defines the term "set" and assigns a brief description. The term is given the label set. This is the minimum amount of information you must give:

Input ↑
```
\newglossaryentry{set}% the label
{%
   name={set},% the term
   description={a collection of objects}% a brief description
}
```
Input ↓

The following entry also has an associated symbol:

Input ↑
```
\newglossaryentry{U}% the label
{%
   name={universal set},% the term
   description={the set of all things},% a brief description
   symbol={\ensuremath{\mathcal{U}}}% the associate symbol
}
```
Input ↓

The plural of the word "matrix" is "matrices" not "matrixs", so the term needs the plural form set explicitly:

Input ↑
```
\newglossaryentry{matrix}% the label
{name={matrix},% the term
 description={a rectangular table of elements},% brief description
 plural={matrices}% the plural
}
```
Input ↓

The glossaries package also provides the shortcut command:

Definition   \newacronym[⟨*key-val list*⟩]{⟨*label*⟩}{⟨*abbrv*⟩}{⟨*long*⟩}

The default behaviour of this command is equivalent to:

```
\newglossaryentry{⟨label⟩}{name={⟨abbrv⟩},description={⟨long⟩},text=
{⟨abbrv⟩},first={⟨long⟩ (⟨abbrv⟩)},plural={⟨abbrv⟩s},firstplural={⟨long⟩s
(⟨abbrv⟩s)},⟨key-val list⟩}
```
↑ Input

↓ Input

EXAMPLE:

```
\newacronym{svm}{SVM}{support vector machine}
```
Input

is equivalent to

```
\newglossaryentry{svm}% the label
{%
   name={SVM},%
   description={support vector machine},%
   first={support vector machine (SVM)},%
   firstplural={support vector machines (SVMs)},%
   text={SVM},%
   plural={SVMs}%
}
```
↑ Input

↓ Input

There are some package options that modify the behaviour of \newacronym. For example, the package option description changes \newacronym so that you need to explicitly set the description in the optional argument. For example:

```
\usepackage[description]{glossaries}

\newacronym[description={a statistical pattern recognition
technique}]{svm}{SVM}{support vector machine}
```
↑ Input

↓ Input

Another package option is footnote which will modify the behaviour of \newacronym so that the long form is displayed as a footnote on first use. For a full list of available options, see the glossaries documentation [16].

Displaying Terms in the Document

Any glossary term that has been defined using \newglossaryentry or \newacronym, as described above, can be displayed in the document using one of the commands described in this section. (There are other less commonly used commands available as well, see the glossaries documentation [16] for details of them.)

Each term has an associated *first use flag*. This is a boolean (true/false) switch that determines whether or not the entry has been used. This is how the glossaries package determines whether to display the value of the first key or to display the value of the text key. You can reset this flag using:

Definition   \glsreset{⟨*label*⟩}

Conversely, you can unset it using:

Definition   \glsunset{⟨*label*⟩}

To display a term that has previously been defined using either \newglossaryentry or \newacronym you can use one of the following commands:

Definition   \gls[⟨*options*⟩]{⟨*label*⟩}[⟨*insert*⟩]

Definition   \glspl[⟨*options*⟩]{⟨*label*⟩}[⟨*insert*⟩]

Definition   \Gls[⟨*options*⟩]{⟨*label*⟩}[⟨*insert*⟩]

Definition   \Glspl[⟨*options*⟩]{⟨*label*⟩}[⟨*insert*⟩]

These commands all have the same syntax: ⟨*label*⟩ is the label that uniquely identifies the term (as supplied in \newglossaryentry or \newacronym), ⟨*insert*⟩ is additional text to insert after the term (but inside the hyperlink, if used with the hyperref package), and ⟨*options*⟩ is a ⟨*key*⟩=⟨*value*⟩ list of options. Available options are:

- format

  This specifies how to format the associated location for this entry. It is analogous to the | special character used in \index (see Section 6.1.1). As with \index, the format must not include the initial backslash. For example, format=textbf indicates that the location should be displayed in bold. (If you are using the hyperref package, you should use the hyper⟨*xx*⟩ formats instead, such as hyperbf, see the glossaries documentation [16] for further detail.)

- counter

  This specifies which counter to use for the associated location in the glossary. This is usually the page number, but can be changed to, say, the section in which the term is used.

- hyper

  This is a boolean key which can be used to enable/disable the hyperlink to the relevant entry in the glossary. Note that setting hyper=true will only have an effect if hyperlinks are supported (through loading the hyperref package before loading the glossaries package). The above commands all have starred versions that are a shortcut for hyper=false. For example \gls*{svm} is equivalent to \gls[hyper=false]{svm}.

The above commands \gls and \Gls will display the value of the first or text key, depending on whether or not the entry has already been used. Similarly, \glspl and \Glspl will display the value of the firstplural or plural key, depending on whether or not the entry has already been used. The upper case forms, \Gls and \Glspl, will capitalise the first letter.

EXAMPLE:
Suppose I have defined the following entry:

```
\newglossaryentry{matrix}% the label
{name={matrix},% the term
 description={a rectangular table of elements},% brief description
 plural={matrices}% the plural
}
```

↑ Input

↓ Input

Then (later in the document)

```
\Glspl{matrix} are usually denoted by a bold capital letter, such as
$\mathbf{A}$. The \gls{matrix}['s] $(i,j)$th element is usually denoted
$a_{ij}$. \Gls{matrix} $\mathbf{I}$ is the identity \gls{matrix}.
```

↑ Input

↓ Input

will display:

Matrices are usually denoted by a bold capital letter, such as **A**. The matrix's (i, j)th element is usually denoted a_{ij}. Matrix **I** is the identity matrix.

↑ Output

↓ Output

If you have used the symbol key when you defined a term, you can access its value with:

\glssymbol[⟨*options*⟩]{⟨*label*⟩}[⟨*insert*⟩]

Definition

This has the same syntax as commands like \gls but it doesn't affect or query the first use flag.

Terms that have been defined using \newacronym can also be referenced using the commands:

\acrshort[⟨*options*⟩]{⟨*label*⟩}[⟨*insert*⟩]
\Acrshort[⟨*options*⟩]{⟨*label*⟩}[⟨*insert*⟩]

Definition

\acrlong[⟨*options*⟩]{⟨*label*⟩}[⟨*insert*⟩]
\Acrlong[⟨*options*⟩]{⟨*label*⟩}[⟨*insert*⟩]

Definition

\acrfull[⟨*options*⟩]{⟨*label*⟩}[⟨*insert*⟩]
\Acrfull[⟨*options*⟩]{⟨*label*⟩}[⟨*insert*⟩]

Definition

These commands don't affect the first use flag. The first two (\acrshort and \Acrshort) will display the abbreviation only, the middle two (\acrlong and \Acrlong) will display the long form only, and the last two (\acrfull and \Acrfull) display both the long and short form. These commands have the same syntax as \gls and \Gls.

If you find these commands a little long-winded to type, you can use the package option shortcuts, which will provide shorter synonyms, such as \acs, \acl and \acf. This option also defines \ac which is equivalent to \gls. See the glossaries user guide [16] for further details.

ANOTHER EXAMPLE:

Suppose I have defined an acronym as follows:

Input   \newacronym{svm}{SVM}{support vector machine}

Then (later in the document):

Input ⊤
Input ⊥
```
First use: \gls{svm}\@. Next use: \gls{svm}\@. Short: \acrshort{svm}\@.
Long: \acrlong{svm}. Full: \acrfull{svm}\@.
```

produces:

Output ⊤
Output ⊥
> First use: support vector machine (SVM). Next use: SVM. Short: SVM. Long: support vector machine. Full: support vector machine (SVM).

(Recall \@ from Volume 1 [15, §2.13].)

NOTE:

Avoid using commands like \gls in section headings or captions. Instead, use commands like:

Definition   \glsentrytext{⟨*label*⟩}

(displays the value of the text key without a hyperlink) or

Definition   \glsentryfirst{⟨*label*⟩}

(displays the value of the first key without a hyperlink). These commands don't affect the first use flag. For related commands, see the glossaries user guide [16].

Take care if you want to use the uppercase variants, such as \Gls or \Acrlong. If the first letter is an accent (either entered using accents commands such as \'{e} or entered directly such as é with the inputenc package) then you must group that letter when you define the term.

EXAMPLE:

⌃ Input

```
\newglossaryentry{elite}% label
{%
  name={{é}lite},%
  description={select group or class}%
}
```

⌄ Input

Defining New Glossaries

If you want the list of acronyms to be separate from the main glossary, you need to use the package option acronym. This will change the effect of \newacronym so that it adds the term to the list of acronyms instead of to the main glossary.

You can also define your own custom glossaries using

$\newglossary[\langle log\text{-}ext\rangle]\{\langle name\rangle\}\{\langle in\text{-}ext\rangle\}\{\langle out\text{-}ext\rangle\}\{\langle title\rangle\}[\langle counter\rangle]$ Definition

where $\langle name\rangle$ is a label that uniquely defines this new glossary and $\langle title\rangle$ is the title to be used when the glossary is displayed in the document via \printglossary or \printglossaries, see Section 6.1.2. The other mandatory arguments, $\langle in\text{-}ext\rangle$ and $\langle out\text{-}ext\rangle$, specify the file extensions to give to the input and output files for this new glossary. The first optional argument $\langle log\text{-}ext\rangle$ is the extension for the log file. This information is provided for the benefit of the makeglossaries application. The final optional argument $\langle counter\rangle$ is the name of the counter used by default in the location lists for this new glossary. If omitted, the page counter is used (unless overridden by the counter package option).

NOTE:

All glossaries must be defined before \makeglossaries to ensure that the relevant output files are opened.

EXAMPLE:

The following defines a new glossary called "notation":

`\newglossary[nlg]{notation}{not}{ntn}{Notation}`   Input

When it gets displayed (using \printglossary or \printglossaries) the title will default to "Notation". I now need to use the type key if I want to define an entry to go in this new glossary:

⌃ Input

```
\newglossaryentry{not:set}% label
{%
  type=notation,% glossary type
  name={$\mathcal{S}$},%
```

```
    description={A set},%
    sort={S}%
}
```

Later in the document I can use this entry:

`A \gls{not:set} is a collection of objects.`

Displaying Glossaries

Now that you know how to define entries and how to use them in the document text, let's now look at the more complicated task of displaying the glossaries. To display all the defined glossaries use:

`\printglossaries`

To only display a particular glossary use:

`\printglossary[⟨options⟩]`

where ⟨options⟩ is a comma-separated list of ⟨key⟩=⟨value⟩ options. Available keys:

- `type`

  The glossary to print. If omitted, the main (default) glossary is assumed.

- `style`

  The glossary style to use. There are a lot of predefined styles to choose from, such as `list`, `long` or `tree`. See the glossaries user manual [16] for further details.

- `title`

  Overrides the default title for this glossary.

- `toctitle`

  Overrides the default title for the table of contents.

- `numberedsection`

  Put this glossary in a numbered section (instead of an unnumbered section).

- `nonumberlist`

  Suppress the location lists for this glossary.

NOTE:
By default, the glossaries aren't added to the table of contents. If you want them added to the table of contents use the package option `toc`.

```
\usepackage[toc]{glossaries}
```
Input

Only those entries that have been used in the document (via commands like \gls) are displayed in the glossary. If you want to add an entry without displaying it in the document, use

```
\glsadd[⟨options⟩]{⟨label⟩}
```
Definition

where ⟨*label*⟩ is the unique label identifying the entry. The optional argument ⟨*options*⟩ is the same as for commands like \gls except there is no hyper key.

Alternatively, you can add all defined entries using:

```
\glsaddall[⟨options⟩]
```
Definition

where ⟨*options*⟩ is the same as for \glsadd except that there is also a types key where the value should be a comma-separated list of all the glossaries to iterate over. For example, to add all entries defined in the "acronym" glossary and the "notation" glossary, but not the "main" glossary:

```
\glsaddall[types={acronym,notation}]
```
Input

NOTE:
As with \printindex the glossaries won't be displayed until the relevant files have been created either by makeindex or by xindy. Unlike in Section 6.1.1, if you want to use xindy to create your glossary files, you can't use the texindy wrapper but must either use xindy directly or use the makeglossaries wrapper, described below. If you want to use xindy with the glossaries package, you must use the xindy package option:

```
\usepackage[xindy]{glossaries}
```
Input

If omitted, makeindex will be assumed.

If you have Perl installed, you can use the makeglossaries application that comes with the glossaries package. If you have been using latexmk or xindy, then you already have Perl installed. If you don't want to install Perl for some reason, there's a Java alternative to makeglossaries called makeglossariesgui that's available from CTAN [2]. However, if you don't install Perl, you are restricting your options as you won't be able to use xindy[6.4].

If you are using arara (see Section 1.1.2), then all you need to do is add another % arara: directive in your source code:

```
% arara: makeglossaries
```
Input

If you are using latexmk, then make sure you have added the custom dependencies for .gls as described in Section 1.1.1. If you are not using any automated tool to build your document, you will have to invoke makeglossaries between (PDF)LATEX runs (see Section 1.1).

Adding to Listing 19 on page 86:

[6.4]or a lot of other useful Perl scripts, such as epstopdf

Listing 20[6.5]

```
% In the preamble:
% arara: pdflatex: { synctex: on }
% arara: biber
% arara: makeglossaries
% arara: makeindex
% arara: pdflatex: { synctex: on }
% arara: pdflatex: { synctex: on }
\documentclass[oneside,12pt]{scrbook}

\usepackage[toc,acronym]{glossaries}

\newglossary[nlg]{notation}{not}{ntn}{Notation}

\makeglossaries

\newglossaryentry{matrix}% the label
{name={matrix},% the term
 description={a rectangular table of elements},% brief description
 plural={matrices}% the plural
}

\newacronym{svm}{SVM}{support vector machine}

\newglossaryentry{not:set}% label
{%
  type=notation,% glossary type
  name={$\mathcal{S}$},%
  description={A set},%
  sort={S}%
}

% Later in the document:

\Glspl{matrix} are usually denoted by a bold capital letter, such as
$\mathbf{A}$. The \gls{matrix}['s] $(i,j)$th element is usually denoted
$a_{ij}$. \Gls{matrix} $\mathbf{I}$ is the identity \gls{matrix}.

First use: \gls{svm}\@. Next use: \gls{svm}\@. Short: \acrshort{svm}\@.
Long: \acrlong{svm}. Full: \acrfull{svm}\@.

A \gls{not:set} is a collection of objects.
```

[6.5]http://www.dickimaw-books.com/latex/thesis/html/examples/thesis-glossaries.tex

```
% At the end of the document:

\backmatter

\printglossaries
```

⤓ Input

Troubleshooting

If you run into difficulties with the glossaries package, first consult the glossaries FAQ[6.6]. You can also check my bug tracker[6.7] if you think you've stumbled on a bug. If you are using TeXnicCenter instead of TeXworks, there are instructions on how to get TeXnicCenter to run makeglossaries in an article I wrote on the LaTeX Community's Know How section [13].

If you're completely confused about how to generate the glossary files, you might want to consider using datagidx instead, described next.

6.2. Using LaTeX to Sort and Collate Indexes or Glossaries (datagidx package)

Section 6.1 described how to create an index or glossaries using an external indexing application. Some users stumble when it comes to invoking the indexing application. There is an alternative where TeX does the sorting and collating. This by-passes the need to use makeindex, xindy or makeglossaries, but it's less efficient and takes longer to build your document. This section describes how to do this using the datagidx package. This package comes with my datatool bundle (at least version 2.13). The documentation for datagidx is included in the datatool user manual [17].

The datatool package allows you to define databases that you can access in your document. The datagidx package has a special interface to this facility that allows you to define databases for the purposes of indexing. These databases and their definitions must be defined in the preamble. In this section, the term "indexing" will be used to refer to either indexes or glossaries, as the same mechanism is used for both tasks.

A new indexing database is defined using:

`\newgidx{⟨label⟩}{⟨title⟩}`

Definition

where ⟨label⟩ is a label that uniquely identifies this database and ⟨title⟩ is the title to be used when the index (or glossary) is displayed. For example:

`\newgidx{index}{Index}`

Input

[6.6] http://www.dickimaw-books.com/faqs/glossariesfaq.html

[6.7] http://www.dickimaw-books.com/cgi-bin/bugtracker.cgi?category=glossaries

creates a new database labelled `index`. When the index is displayed, it will have the section heading "Index".

As in Section 6.1, each term in the index (or glossary) database has an associated location list. This list is initially null. The locations are added to terms used in the document on *the second* LaTeX *run*. When you display the index, only those entries with a non-null location list or a cross-reference will be shown. The default location is the page number on which the entry was referenced. The datagidx package knows about the following page numbering styles: `arabic`, `roman`, `Roman`, `alph` and `Alph`. If your document has another type of numbering style, or if you want to use a different counter for the location, consult the datagidx section of the datatool manual [17].

Once you have defined the indexing database, you can now define terms associated with that database using

Definition   `\newterm[`⟨*options*⟩`]{`⟨*name*⟩`}`

where ⟨*name*⟩ is the term and ⟨*options*⟩ is a list of ⟨*key*⟩=⟨*value*⟩ options. The following keys are available:

- `database`

  Identifies the database in which to store this term. For example:

Definition   `\newterm[database=index]{eigenvalue}`

It can be somewhat cumbersome having to type the database for each new term. Instead you can define the default database using:

Definition   `\DTLgidxSetDefaultDB{`⟨*label*⟩`}`

For example:

Input ⊤

```
\newgidx{index}{Index}
\DTLgidxSetDefaultDB{index}

\newterm{eigenvalue}
\newterm{eigenvector}
```

Input ⊥

- `label`

  A label uniquely identifying this term. If omitted the label is extracted from ⟨*name*⟩.

- `sort`

  The sort key. If omitted this is extracted from ⟨*name*⟩.

- parent

  The parent entry, if this is a sub-term. (The value should be the label identifying the parent, which must already be defined.)

- text

  How the entry should appear in the document text. If omitted, ⟨*name*⟩ is used. If present, ⟨*name*⟩ indicates how the term should appear in the index/glossary.

- description

  An optional associated description.

- plural

  The plural form of this term. If omitted this value is obtained by appending "s" to ⟨*name*⟩ (or the value of text if supplied).

- symbol

  An optional associated symbol.

- short

  An associated short form, if required. (Defaults to ⟨*name*⟩ if omitted.)

- long

  An associated long form, if required. (Defaults to ⟨*name*⟩ if omitted.)

- shortplural

  The plural of the associated short form. If omitted, the value is obtained by appending "s" to the short form.

- longplural

  The plural of the associated long form. If omitted, the value is obtained by appending "s" to the long form.

- see

  A cross-reference to a synonym. The value should be the label of another entry. This entry will not have a location list, just the reference to the other term.

- seealso

  A cross-reference to a closely related term. Both this term and the cross-referenced term should have a location list.

It's also possible to add your own custom keys. See the datagidx section of the datatool user guide [17] for further details.

As with \newglossaryentry, discussed in Section 6.1.2, if the term starts with an accented letter (or a ligature) the letter must be grouped.

EXAMPLE:

Input ↑

```
\newterm[label=elite,sort=elite]{{é}lite}

\newterm
 [%
    plural={{œ}sophagi},
    label={oesophagus},
    sort={oesophagus},
    description={tube connecting throat and stomach}
 ]
 {{œ}sophagus}
```

Input ↓

There is a shortcut command for defining acronyms:

Definition   `\newacro[⟨options⟩]{⟨short⟩}{⟨long⟩}`

where ⟨*short*⟩ is the abbreviation and ⟨*long*⟩ is the long form. The optional argument ⟨*options*⟩ is the same as for \newterm. This is equivalent to:

```
\newterm
 [%
    description={\capitalisewords{⟨long⟩}},%
    short={\acronymfont{⟨short⟩}},%
    long={⟨long⟩},%
    text={\DTLgidxAcrStyle{⟨long⟩}{\acronymfont{⟨short⟩}}},%
    plural={\DTLgidxAcrStyle{⟨long⟩s}{\acronymfont{⟨short⟩s}}},%
    sort={⟨short⟩},%
    ⟨options⟩%
 ]%
 {\MakeTextUppercase{⟨short⟩}}
```

where

Definition   `\DTLgidxAcrStyle{⟨long⟩}{⟨short⟩}`

formats the full version of the acronym. This defaults to: ⟨*long*⟩ (⟨*short*⟩), and

Definition   `\acronymfont{⟨text⟩}`

is the font used to format acronyms. By default this just displays its argument, but can be redefined if you want the acronyms formatted in a particular style or font (such as small-caps). The other commands used above are:

Definition   `\MakeTextUppercase{⟨text⟩}`

This is defined by the textcase package and converts ⟨*text*⟩ to uppercase.

`\capitalisewords{⟨text⟩}` Definition

This is defined by the mfirstuc package and capitalises the first letter of each word in ⟨*text*⟩.

EXAMPLE:

`\newacro{svm}{support vector machine}` Input

Once you have defined the terms in the preamble, you can later use them in the document:

`\gls{[⟨format⟩]⟨label⟩}` Definition

`\glspl{[⟨format⟩]⟨label⟩}` Definition

`\Gls{[⟨format⟩]⟨label⟩}` Definition

`\Glspl{[⟨format⟩]⟨label⟩}` Definition

These are similar to those described in Section 6.1.2, but they have a different syntax. Here ⟨*format*⟩ is the name of a text-block commands (such as `\textbf`) *without* the initial backslash that should be used to format the location for this reference. This is analogous to the | special character described in Section 6.1.1.

There are also commands associated with acronyms:

`\acr{[⟨format⟩]⟨label⟩}` Definition

`\acrpl{[⟨format⟩]⟨label⟩}` Definition

`\Acr{[⟨format⟩]⟨label⟩}` Definition

`\Acrpl{[⟨format⟩]⟨label⟩}` Definition

Unlike the glossaries package, described in Section 6.1.2, there is a difference between datagidx's `\gls` and `\acr`. Here `\gls` will always display the value of the text field, whereas `\acr` will display the full form on first use (the text field) and the abbreviation on subsequent use (the short field).

You can also add terms to the index without creating any link text:

`\glsadd{⟨label⟩}` Definition

This adds the term uniquely identified by ⟨*label*⟩.

Definition   \glsaddall{⟨*database name*⟩}

This adds all the terms defined in the database uniquely identified by ⟨*database name*⟩.

NOTE:

Unlike most commands, the optional part of the above commands occurs *inside* the mandatory argument.

EXAMPLES:

Given the `elite` and `oesophagus` examples defined on page 102, I can reference those entries in the text as follows:

Input   \Gls{elite} and \glspl{oesophagus}.

This produces:

Output   Élite and œsophagi.

Elsewhere, I might have the main topic about œsophagi:

Input ↑
Input ↓
```
The \gls{[textbf]oesophagus} connects the throat and the stomach.
```

This produces:

Output   The œsophagus connects the throat and the stomach.

and the associated location will be typeset in bold.

Here's an example using the `svm` example defined on the preceding page:

Input ↑
Input ↓
```
First use: \acr{svm}\@. Subsequent use: \acr{svm}\@. Full form:
\gls{svm}.
```

This produces:

Output ↑
Output ↓
> First use: support vector machine (SVM). Subsequent use: SVM. Full form: support vector machine (SVM).

You can unset and reset acronyms using

Definition   \glsunset{⟨*label*⟩}

and

Definition   \glsreset{⟨*label*⟩}

To display the index or glossary or list of acronyms use:

Definition   \printterms[⟨*options*⟩]

where ⟨*options*⟩ is a comma-separated ⟨*key*⟩=⟨*value*⟩ list. Common options are:

- database

  The label uniquely identifying the database containing the relevant terms.

- postdesc

  This may have the value dot (put a full stop after the description, if there is a description) or none (don't put a full stop after the description).

- columns

  This value must be an integer greater than or equal to 1, indicating the number of columns for the page layout.

- style

  The style to use. There are a number of predefined styles, such as index or gloss. See the user guide [17] for further details.

- namecase

  Indicates whether any case change should be applied to the entry's name. Available values are: nochange (no change), uc (convert to uppercase), lc (convert to lower case), firstuc (convert the first letter to uppercase) and capitalise (capitalise each initial letter using \capitalisewords).

For a full list of options see the datagidx section of the datatool user guide [17].

Listing 20 on page 98 can now be rewritten as follows:

Listing 21[6.8]

↑ Input

```
% arara: pdflatex: { synctex: on }
% arara: biber
% arara: pdflatex: { synctex: on }
% arara: pdflatex: { synctex: on }
\documentclass[oneside,12pt]{scrbook}

\usepackage{datagidx}

\newgidx{index}{Index}
\newgidx{glossary}{Glossary}
\newgidx{acronym}{Acronyms}
\newgidx{notation}{Notation}

\DTLgidxSetDefaultDB{glossary}

\newterm
 [%
   description={a rectangular table of elements},% brief description
   plural={matrices}% the plural
```

[6.8] http://www.dickimaw-books.com/latex/thesis/html/examples/thesis-datagidx.tex

```
  ]%
  {matrix}% the name

\DTLgidxSetDefaultDB{acronym}

\newacro{svm}{support vector machine}

\DTLgidxSetDefaultDB{notation}

\newterm
  [%
   label={not:set},% label
   description={A set},%
   sort={S}%
  ]%
  {\ensuremath{\mathcal{S}}}}

\DTLgidxSetDefaultDB{index}

\newterm
  [%
    label={function},%
    text={function}%
  ]%
  {functions}

\newterm
  [%
    see={sqrt},%
  ]%
  {square root}

\newterm
  [%
    label={fn.sqrt},
    parent={function}
  ]%
  {\texttt{sqrt()}}

\newterm
  [%
    label={sqrt},
  ]%
  {sqrt()}
```

```
\newterm{tautology}
\newterm{contradiction}

% later in the document:

\Glspl{matrix} are usually denoted by a bold capital letter, such as
$\mathbf{A}$. The \gls{matrix}'s $(i,j)$th element is usually denoted
$a_{ij}$. \Gls{matrix} $\mathbf{I}$ is the identity \gls{matrix}.

First use: \acr{svm}\@. Next use: \acr{svm}\@. Full: \gls{svm}\@.

A \gls{not:set} is a collection of objects.

...

Some sample code is shown in Listing~\ref{lst:sample}. This uses the
function \gls{fn.sqrt}.\glsadd{sqrt}

...

\begin{Definition}[Tautology]
A \emph{\gls[[textbf]tautology}} is a proposition that is always true for
any value of its variables.
\end{Definition}

\begin{Definition}[Contradiction]
A \emph{\gls[[textbf]contradiction}} is a proposition that is always
false for any value of its variables.
\end{Definition}

% At the end of the document:
\backmatter

\printterms[database=glossary]
\printterms[database=acronym]
\printterms[database=notation]

\printbibliography

\printterms[database=index]
```

⤓ Input

Note that there is now no need to call either makeindex or makeglossaries. The only external application being called is biber for the bibliography.

Appendix A

General Advice

If you encounter any LATEX problems, check Appendix B (Common Errors) and Appendix C (Need More Help?) in *LATEX for Complete Novices* [15].

A.1. Too Many Unprocessed Floats

A common problem PhD student's encounter when writing a thesis is the "too many unprocessed floats" error. This is usually caused by having too many figures and tables in the results chapter and not enough surrounding text. If this happens, there are a number of things you can try doing:

[FAQ: Too many unprocessed floats]

1. Make sure you haven't been too restrictive in where you want your floats to go. If you use a placement specifier, give LaTeX as many options as possible. For example:

   `\begin{figure}[htbp]`   Input

   which indicates that the figure can be placed "here" (h), at the top of a page (t), at the bottom of the page (b) or on a page solely consisting of floats (p). If you just use the h placement specifier then you are stating: "I want it *here* and *nowhere else!*" If TEX can't put it *exactly here*, then you have given no alternative place to put it, and it won't get placed anywhere, unless a `\clearpage` command is issued, at which point all remaining unprocessed floats will be dumped at that point. If you are determined that an image must be placed *exactly here* then it should not be placed in a floating environment.

2. Try increasing the amount of text in the chapter. Remember that you should never simply print all the figures and tables in a results chapter without discussing them to some extent.

3. If all else fails, try using the `\clearpage` command. This forces all unprocessed floats to be processed immediately, and start a new page. This may result in the page ending prematurely, if you wish to avoid this, you can use the afterpage package, and use the command:

   `\afterpage{\clearpage}`   Input

For other problems, check the FAQ [19].

A.2. General Thesis Writing Advice

This section is not specific to LaTeX. Some of the points have already been mentioned in asides or footnotes. Remember that each college or university or even school within a university may have different requirements, and requirements will also vary according to country, so some of this advice may not apply to you. I am writing from the point of view of an English scientist, and am basing it on my own experience and on the comments of English science-based PhD examiners and supervisors. I cannot guarantee that your own department or university will agree with them. *If in doubt, check with your supervisor.*

1. Find out the thesis style requirements from your supervisor or your department's website. Many universities still require double-spaced, single-sided documents with wide margins. Double-spacing is by and large looked down on in the world of typesetting, but this requirement for a PhD thesis has nothing to do with æsthetics or readability. In England the purpose of the PhD viva is to defend your work[A.1]. Before your viva, paper copies of your thesis are sent to your examiners. The double spacing and wide margins provide the examiners room to write the comments and criticisms they wish to raise during the viva, as well as any typographical corrections. Whilst they could write these comments on a separate piece of paper, cross-referencing the page in the thesis, it is more efficient for the comments to actually be on the relevant page of the thesis. That way, as they go through the manuscript during your viva, they can easily see the comments, questions or criticisms they wish to raise alongside the corresponding text. If you present them with a single-spaced document with narrow margins, you are effectively telling them that you don't want them to criticise your work!

2. Don't try to pad your thesis with irrelevant information. This includes adding items in your bibliography that are not referenced in the text, adding figures or tables that are not explained in the text, and supplying all the source code you have written. The outcome of your viva will not depend on the physical size of your thesis, but on the clarity of your writing and on the quality of your work.

3. Clearly delineate your thesis through the use of chapters and sections, outlining your original aims and objectives, an overview of the subject matter including references to other people's work in the area, the methods you employed to extend or innovate the field, your results and conclusions.

4. Make sure your references include some recent journal or conference papers to illustrate that you are aware of new developments in your field. Remember that due to the nature of publishing, most books are dated by the time they

---

[A.1]I gather this is not the case in some other countries, where the viva is more informal, and the decision to pass or fail you has already been made before your viva.

reach the book shelves. Journal and conference papers are likely to be more up-to-date[A.2].

5. Always explain acronyms, technical terms and symbols. It is a good idea to include a glossary of terms, list of notation or list of acronyms to avoid confusion (see Chapter 6 (Generating Indexes and Glossaries)).

6. If you have equations, make sure you explain the variables used, and how you go from one equation to the next. Depending on your field, you might also consider clarifying the mathematics by providing graphical representations of the equations[A.3].

7. If you include any graphs, bar charts, pie charts or any other form of data plot, make sure it is clearly labelled and no distortion is introduced (such as using three-dimensional bar charts or pie charts[A.4].)

8. If you have used a computer application to generate numerical results, make sure you have some understanding of the underlying process and what the results mean. This doesn't necessarily mean that you need to understand complex computer code, or complex algorithms, but what you shouldn't do is say something along the lines of, "well, I clicked on this button, and it said $m = 0.678$." What is the purpose of the button? What does m represent? What does the result $m = 0.678$ signify? What value were you expecting or hoping to get? Numbers on their own are meaningless. If I ran into a room shouting "I've got 42!" What does that mean? Forty-two what? Forty-two brilliant reviews? (Great!) Forty-two percent in an exam? (Not good.) Forty-two spots on my face? (Very bad!)

9. Don't waste time worrying about the best way to word your thesis in your first draft. Write first, then edit it later or you will never get started.

10. If your supervisor offers to critique chapters of your thesis, don't say no! Such offers are not made out of politeness, but a desire to ensure that you pass. Don't be embarrassed and worry that it's not good enough, that's the whole point in your supervisor helping you improve it[A.5].

11. Write in a clear concise manner. A thesis is a technical document, not a novel, so don't be tempted to write something along the lines of: "I awaited with bated breath, my whole body quivering with excitement at the eager anticipation that

---

[A.2]Having said that, I know someone who submitted an article to a journal, and it took three and a half years before the reviewers came back with comments. In the end, the author withdrew the manuscript because by that time the topic was out of date.

[A.3]When I was a PhD student, I was once rendered speechless when asked to provide a graphical illustration of an equation involving a quadruple summation that had no graphical meaning from my point of view. Perhaps this was a drawback of being a mathematician doing a PhD in an electronics department.

[A.4]The sole purpose of 3D pie charts or bar charts appears to be to look pretty and impress people who have no understanding of mathematics.

[A.5]but don't expect your supervisor to actually write your thesis!

my algorithm would prove superior to all others, and, oh joy, my experiments proved me right."

12. Don't decorate your thesis with irrelevant clip art. It is unprofessional and highly inappropriate in the sciences.

13. Make regular backups of your work. Be prepared for any of the following: accidentally deleting your thesis, accidentally overwriting your thesis with another file, software failure, hardware failure, viruses, fire and theft. Consider using at least a two-tier system where you keep one backup in a safe place where you live and ask a close relative or friend to take care of another backup.

Items 9 and 10 above were supplied by Dr Gavin Cawley[A.6] who has been both a PhD supervisor and examiner.

[A.6] School of Computing Sciences, University of East Anglia

Bibliography

[1] John Collins, Evan McLean, and David J. Musliner. latexmk—generate LaTeX document, 2012. http://mirror.ctan.org/support/latexmk/latexmk.pdf or texdoc latexmk.

[2] The comprehensive TeX archive network. http://mirror.ctan.org/.

[3] Jürgen Fenn. The TeX catalogue online, topic index. http://mirror.ctan.org/help/Catalogue/bytopic.html.

[4] Christophe Fiorio. algorithm2e.sty —package for algorithms, 2013. http://mirror.ctan.org/macros/latex/contrib/algorithm2e/doc/algorithm2e.pdf or texdoc algorithm2e.

[5] LaTeX for Humans. Thesis and dissertation templates for LaTeX, 2011. http://latexforhumans.wordpress.com/2011/03/10/thesis-templates-for-latex/.

[6] Carsten Heinz and Brooks Moses. The listings package, 2007. http://mirror.ctan.org/macros/latex/contrib/listings/listings.pdf or texdoc listings.

[7] Philip Kime and François Charette. biber: A backend bibliography processor for biblatex, 2012. http://mirror.ctan.org/biblio/biber/documentation/biber.pdf or texdoc biber.

[8] Markus Kohm and Jens-Uwe Morawski. KOMA-Script a versatile LaTeX2ε bundle, 2012. http://mirror.ctan.org/macros/latex/contrib/koma-script/doc/scrguien.pdf or texdoc koma.

[9] Philipp Lehman, Audrey Boruvka, Philip Kime, and Joseph Wright. The biblatex package, 2013. http://mirror.ctan.org/macros/latex/contrib/biblatex/doc/biblatex.pdf or texdoc biblatex.

[10] Wolfgang May and Andreas Schedler. An extension of the LaTeX-theorem environment, 2011. http://mirror.ctan.org/macros/latex/contrib/ntheorem/ntheorem.pdf or texdoc ntheorem.

[11] Oren Patashnik. BibTeXing, 1988. http://mirror.ctan.org/biblio/bibtex/base/btxhak.pdf or texdoc bibtex.

[12] R. M. Ritter. *Oxford Style Manual*. Oxford University Press, 2003.

[13] Nicola Talbot. Glossaries, nomenclature, lists of symbols and acronyms. *The LaTeX Community's Know How Section*, March 2009. http://www.latex-community.org/know-how/latex/55-latex-general/263-glossaries-nomenclature-lists-of-symbols-and-acronyms.

[14] Nicola L. C. Talbot. *Creating a PDF Document Using PDFLaTeX*, volume 4 of *Dickimaw LaTeX Series*. Dickmaw Books, 2004. http://www.dickimaw-books.com/latex/pdfdoc/.

[15] Nicola L. C. Talbot. *LaTeX for Complete Novices*, volume 1 of *Dickimaw LaTeX Series*. Dickmaw Books, 2012. http://www.dickimaw-books.com/latex/novices/.

[16] Nicola L. C. Talbot. User manual for glossaries.sty, 2012. http://mirror.ctan.org/macros/latex/contrib/glossaries/glossaries-user.pdf or texdoc glossaries-user.

[17] Nicola L. C. Talbot. User manual for datatool bundle, 2013. http://mirror.ctan.org/macros/latex/contrib/datatool/datatool-user.pdf or texdoc datatool-user.

[18] Mark Trettin and Jürgen Fenn. An essential guide to LaTeX 2_ε usage: obsolete commands and packages, 2007. http://mirror.ctan.org/info/l2tabu/english or texdoc l2tabu-en.

[19] UK list of TeX frequently asked questions. http://www.tex.ac.uk/faq or texdoc faq.

[20] Joseph Wright. siunitx — a comprehensive (SI) units package, 2013. http://mirror.ctan.org/macros/latex/contrib/siunitx/siunitx.pdf or texdoc siunitx.

ACRONYMS

CTAN The Comprehensive TeX Archive Network. http://mirror.ctan.org/.

UK FAQ UK List of TeX Frequently Asked Questions. http://www.tex.ac.uk/faq.

Summary of Commands and Environments

Commands or environments defined in the LATEX kernel are always available.

Symbols

!

`makeindex` sublevel special character [§6.1]

␣

A visual indication of a space in the code. When you type up the code, replace all instances of this symbol with a space via the space bar on your keyboard. [§1.0]

"

`makeindex` escape special character [§6.1]

#⟨*digit*⟩

Defined in: LATEX Kernel.

Replacement text for argument ⟨*digit*⟩. (See Volume 1 [15, §8].) [§4.5]

$

Defined in: LATEX Kernel.

Switches in and out of in-line math mode. (See Volume 1 [15, §9.1].) [§4.5]

%

Defined in: LATEX Kernel.

Comment character used to ignore everything up to and including the newline character in the source code. Sometimes comments are used to provide information to applications that build your document, such as arara. [§2.0]

% arara:

Instruction to arara indicating how to build the document. This is ignored if you are not using arara. [§1.1]

'

Defined in: LATEX Kernel.

Closing quote or apostrophe ' symbol in text mode or prime symbol ' in math mode. (See Volume 1 [15, §4.3].) [§4.7]

''

Defined in: LATEX Kernel.

Closing double quote " symbol in text mode or double prime " in math mode. (See Volume 1 [15, §4.3].) [§4.7]

--

Defined in: LATEX Kernel.

En-dash – symbol. (Normally used for number ranges. See Volume 1 [15, §4.3].) [§5.1]

@

Used in the argument of \index to separate the sort key from the term being indexed. [§6.1]

[

Defined in: LATEX Kernel.

Open delimiter of an optional argument. (See Volume 1 [15, §2.8.2].) [§1.0]

****

Defined in: LATEX Kernel.

Escape character indicating
a command. (See Volume 1 [15, §2.6].)
[§6.1]

\"{⟨c⟩}

Defined in: LaTeX Kernel.

Umlaut over ⟨c⟩. Example: \"{o}
produces ö. (See Volume 1 [15, §4.3].)
[§5.1]

\'{⟨c⟩}

Defined in: LaTeX Kernel.

Acute accent over ⟨c⟩. Example: \'{o}
produces ó. (See Volume 1 [15, §4.3].)
[§6.1]

\+

Defined in: tabbing environment.

Shifts the left border by one tab stop to
the right. [§4.6]

\-

Defined in: LaTeX Kernel.

1) Outside tabbing environment inserts a
discretionary hyphen [§4.6]; 2) Inside
tabbing environment shifts the left
border by one tab stop [§4.6].

\;

Defined in: algorithm2e package.

When used in the body of one of the
environments defined by algorithm2e,
such as algorithm, marks the end of the
line. Outside those environments, this
is a math spacing command. [§4.8]

\<

Defined in: tabbing environment.

Jumps to the next tab stop. [§4.6]

\=

Defined in: LaTeX Kernel.

1) Outside tabbing environment puts a
macron accent over the following
character [§4.6]; 2) Inside tabbing
environment sets a tab-stop. [§4.6].

\>

Defined in: tabbing environment.

Jumps to the previous tab stop. [§4.6]

\@

Defined in: LaTeX Kernel.

Used when a sentence ends with a
capital letter. This command should be
placed after the letter and before the
punctuation mark. (See Volume 1 [15,
§2.13].) [§6.1]

\\

Defined in: LaTeX Kernel.

Starts a new row in tabbing or
tabular-style environments. (See
Volume 1 [15, §4.6.1].) [§2.0]

]

Defined in: LaTeX Kernel.

Closing delimiter of an optional
argument. (See Volume 1 [15, §2.8.2].)
[§1.0]

^{⟨maths⟩}

Defined in: LaTeX Kernel (Math Mode).

Displays its argument as a superscript.
(See Volume 1 [15, §9.4.3].) [§4.8]

_{⟨maths⟩}

Defined in: LaTeX Kernel (Math Mode).

Displays its argument as a subscript.
(See Volume 1 [15, §9.4.3].) [§4.8]

''

Defined in: LaTeX Kernel.

Open double quote " symbol. (See
Volume 1 [15, §4.3].) [§4.7]

\"

{

Defined in: LATEX Kernel.

Marks the beginning of a group. (See Volume 1 [15, §2.7].) [§1.0]

|

When used in \index, this symbol indicates that the rest of the argument list is to be used as the encapsulating command for the page number. [§6.1]

}

Defined in: LATEX Kernel.

Marks the end of a group. (See Volume 1 [15, §2.7].) [§1.0]

~

Defined in: LATEX Kernel.

Unbreakable space. (See Volume 1 [15, §4.3].) [§4.7]

A

\a⟨*accent symbol*⟩{⟨*character*⟩}

Defined in: LATEX Kernel.

Used in the tabbing environment to create accented characters. [§4.6]

\begin{abstract}

Defined in: Most article- or report-style classes, such as scrartcl or scrreprt. Not usually defined in book-style classes, such as scrbook, but is defined in memoir.

Displays its contents as an abstract. [§2.0]

\ac[⟨*options*⟩][⟨*label*⟩][⟨*insert*⟩]

Defined in: glossaries package.

A synonym for \gls. This command is only available if the package option shortcuts is used. [§6.1]

\acf[⟨*options*⟩]{⟨*label*⟩}[⟨*insert*⟩]

Defined in: glossaries package.

A synonym for \acrfull. This command is only available if the package option shortcuts is used. [§6.1]

\acl[⟨*options*⟩]{⟨*label*⟩}[⟨*insert*⟩]

Defined in: glossaries package.

A synonym for \acrlong. This command is only available if the package option shortcuts is used. [§6.1]

\Acr{[⟨*format*⟩]⟨*label*⟩}

Defined in: datagidx package.

As \acr but the first letter is converted to uppercase. [§6.2]

\acr{[⟨*format*⟩]⟨*label*⟩}

Defined in: datagidx package.

Displays an acronym. On first use the full form is displayed. On subsequent use only the short form is displayed. [§6.2]

\Acrfull[⟨*options*⟩]{⟨*label*⟩}[⟨*insert*⟩]

Defined in: glossaries package.

Displays the long and short form of the given acronym, the first letter converted to uppercase. [§6.1]

\acrfull[⟨*options*⟩]{⟨*label*⟩}[⟨*insert*⟩]

Defined in: glossaries package.

Displays the long and short form of the given acronym. [§6.1]

\Acrlong[⟨*options*⟩]{⟨*label*⟩}[⟨*insert*⟩]

Defined in: glossaries package.

Displays the long form of the given acronym, the first letter converted to uppercase. [§6.1]

\acrlong[⟨*options*⟩]{⟨*label*⟩}[⟨*insert*⟩]

Defined in: glossaries package.

Displays the long form of the given acronym. [§6.1]

\acronymfont{⟨*text*⟩}

Defined in: glossaries and datagidx packages.

Font used to display acronyms. [§6.2]

\Acrpl{[⟨*format*⟩]⟨*label*⟩}

Defined in: datagidx package.

As \acrpl but the first letter is converted to uppercase. [§6.2]

\acrpl{[⟨*format*⟩]⟨*label*⟩}

Defined in: datagidx package.

Displays the plural of an acronym. On first use the full form is displayed. On subsequent use only the short form is displayed. [§6.2]

\Acrshort[⟨*options*⟩]{⟨*label*⟩}[⟨*insert*⟩]

Defined in: glossaries package.

Displays the short form of the given acronym, the first letter converted to uppercase. [§6.1]

\acrshort[⟨*options*⟩]{⟨*label*⟩}[⟨*insert*⟩]

Defined in: glossaries package.

Displays the short form of the given acronym. [§6.1]

\acs[⟨*options*⟩]{⟨*label*⟩}[⟨*insert*⟩]

Defined in: glossaries package.

A synonym for \acrshort. This command is only available if the package option shortcuts is used. [§6.1]

\addbibresource[⟨*options*⟩]{⟨*resource*⟩}

Defined in: biblatex package.

Adds a resource, such as a .bib file [§5.3]

\addtokomafont{⟨*element name*⟩}{⟨*commands*⟩}

Defined in: scrartcl, scrreprt and scrbook classes.

Sets the font characteristics for the given KOMA-Script element. (See Volume 1 [15, §5.3].) [§4.1]

\AE

Defined in: LaTeX Kernel.

Æ ligature. [§6.1]

\afterpage{⟨*code*⟩}

Defined in: afterpage package.

Indicates code that should be implemented at the next page break. [§1.1]

\begin{algorithm}[⟨*placement*⟩]

Defined in: algorithm2e package.

A floating environment for typesetting algorithms. [§4.8]

\begin{algorithm2e}[⟨*placement*⟩]

Defined in: algorithm2e package.

Replacement for algorithm when used with the algo2e package option. [§4.8]

\ang{⟨*angle*⟩}

Defined in: siunitx package.

Typesets ⟨*angle*⟩ where ⟨*angle*⟩ is a single number or three semi-colon separated values. [§4.9]

\author{⟨*name*⟩}

Defined in: Most classes that have the concept of a title page.

Specifies the document author (or authors). This command doesn't display any text so may be used in the preamble, but if it's not in the preamble it must be placed before \maketitle. [§2.0]

B

\backmatter

Defined in: Most book-style classes, such as scrbook.

Suppresses chapter and section numbering, but still adds unstarred sectional units to the table of contents. (See also \frontmatter and \mainmatter.) [§2.0]

\begin{⟨env-name⟩}[⟨env-option⟩] {⟨env-arg-1⟩}...{⟨env-arg-n⟩}

Defined in: LATEX Kernel.

Starts an environment. (Must have a matching \end. See Volume 1 [15, §2.15].) [§2.0]

\bfseries

Defined in: LATEX Kernel.

Switches to the bold weight in the current font family. (See Volume 1 [15, §4.5.1].) [§4.1]

\bibitem[⟨tag⟩]{⟨key⟩}

Defined in: LATEX Kernel.

Indicates the start of a new reference in the bibliography. May only be used inside the contents of thebibliography environment. (See Volume 1 [15, §5.6].) [§5.1]

\bibliography{⟨bib list⟩}

Defined in: LATEX Kernel.

Inputs the .bbl file (if it exists) and identifies the name(s) of the bibliography database files where the citations are defined. [§5.2]

\bibliographystyle{⟨style-name⟩}

Defined in: LATEX Kernel.

Specifies the bibliography style to be used by bibtex. [§5.2]

C

\capitalisewords{⟨text⟩}

Defined in: mfirstuc package.

Converts the initial letter of each word in ⟨text⟩ to uppercase. [§6.2]

\caption[⟨short caption⟩]{⟨caption text⟩}

Defined in: LATEX Kernel.

Inserts the caption for a float such as a figure or table. (See Volume 1 [15, §7].) [§4.8]

\centering

Defined in: LATEX Kernel.

Switches the paragraph alignment to centred. (See Volume 1 [15, §2.12].) [§4.1]

\cfoot[⟨scrplain⟩]{⟨scrheadings⟩}

Defined in: scrpage2 package.

Indicates what to put in the centre footer area for the scrplain and scrheadings page styles. [§4.2]

\chapter[⟨short title⟩]{⟨title⟩}

Defined in: Book-style classes (such as scrbook or screprt) that have the concept of chapters.

Inserts a chapter heading. [§2.0]

\chead[⟨scrplain⟩]{⟨scrheadings⟩}

Defined in: scrpage2 package.

Indicates what to put in the centre heading area for the scrplain and scrheadings page styles. [§4.2]

\chead

\Cite[⟨*prenote*⟩][⟨*postnote*⟩]{⟨*key*⟩}

Defined in: biblatex package.

Like \cite but for use at the start of a sentence. [§5.3]

\cite[⟨*text*⟩]{⟨*key list*⟩}

Defined in: LaTeX Kernel.

Inserts the citation markers of each reference identified in the key list. A second run is required to ensure the reference is correct. When used with biblatex, this command has two optional arguments. [§5.2]

\citep[⟨*pre*⟩][⟨*post*⟩]{⟨*key*⟩}

Defined in: natbib package.

Parenthetical citation. [§5.2]

\citet[⟨*pre*⟩][⟨*post*⟩]{⟨*key*⟩}

Defined in: natbib package.

Textual citation. [§5.2]

\clearpage

Defined in: LaTeX Kernel.

Inserts a page break and processes any unprocessed floats [§3.0]

D

\date{⟨*text*⟩}

Defined in: Most classes that have the concept of a title page.

Specifies the document date. This command doesn't display any text so may be used in the preamble, but if it's not in the preamble it must be placed before \maketitle. If omitted, most classes assume the current date. [§2.0]

\documentclass[⟨*option-list*⟩]{⟨*class-name*⟩}

Defined in: LaTeX Kernel.

Loads the document class file, which sets up the type of document you wish to write. (See Volume 1 [15, §4].) [§2.0]

\DontPrintSemicolon

Defined in: algorithm2e package.

Switches off the end of line semi-colon. (See also \PrintSemicolon.) [§4.8]

\doublespacing

Defined in: setspace package.

Switches to double line-spacing. [§4.3]

\DTLgidxAcrStyle{⟨*long*⟩}{⟨*short*⟩}

Defined in: datagidx package.

Formats the long and short form of an acronym. [§6.2]

\DTLgidxSetDefaultDB{⟨*database label*⟩}

Defined in: datagidx package.

Sets the default indexing database. [§6.2]

E

\Else{⟨*block*⟩}

Defined in: algorithm2e package.

For use in algorithm-like environments to indicate an else-block [§4.8]

\ElseIf{⟨*block*⟩}

Defined in: algorithm2e package.

For use in algorithm-like environments to indicate an elseif-block [§4.8]

\emph{⟨*text*⟩}

Defined in: LaTeX Kernel.

Toggles the upright and italic/slanted rendering of ⟨*text*⟩. (See Volume 1 [15, §4.5.1].) [§4.7]

\end{⟨*env-name*⟩}

Defined in: LaTeX Kernel.

Ends an environment. (Must have a matching \begin. See Volume 1 [15, §2.15].) [§2.0]

\ensuremath{⟨*maths*⟩}

Defined in: LaTeX Kernel.

Ensures that its argument is displayed in maths mode. (If it's already in maths mode, it just displays its argument, but if it's not already in maths mode, it will typeset its argument in in-line maths mode.) This command is usually only used in definitions, such as in \newglossaryentry, where it may be used in either text or math mode. [§6.1]

\epsilon

Defined in: LaTeX Kernel (Math Mode).

Greek lower case epsilon ϵ. (See Volume 1 [15, §9.4.2].) [§4.8]

\equiv

Defined in: LaTeX Kernel (Math Mode).

Relational $\equiv$ symbol. (See Volume 1 [15, §9.4.7].) [§4.7]

\excludeonly⟨⟨*file list*⟩⟩

Defined in: excludeonly Package.

Lists which of the files that are not to be included using \include. Only those files not in the list will be included. (The opposite effect of \includeonly.) [§3.0]

F

\begin{figure}[⟨*placement*⟩]

Defined in: Most classes that define sectioning commands.

Floats the contents to the nearest location according to the preferred placement options, if possible. Within the environment, \caption may be used one or more times, as required. (See Volume 1 [15, §7.1].) [§4.8]

\For{⟨*condition*⟩}{⟨*body*⟩}

Defined in: algorithm2e package.

For use in algorithm-like environments to indicate a for-loop [§4.8]

\frac{⟨*numerator*⟩}{⟨*denominator*⟩}

Defined in: LaTeX Kernel (Math Mode).

Displays a fraction. (See Volume 1 [15, §9.4.5].) [§4.8]

\frontmatter

Defined in: Most book-style classes, such as scrbook.

Switches to lower case Roman numeral page numbering. Also suppresses chapter and section numbering, but still adds unstarred sectional units to the table of contents. (See also \mainmatter and \backmatter.) [§2.0]

G

\Gls[⟨*options*⟩]{⟨*label*⟩}[⟨*insert*⟩]

Defined in: glossaries package.

Displays a glossary term according to its first use flag. The first letter of the term is converted to uppercase. [§6.1]

\Gls{[⟨*format*⟩]⟨*label*⟩}

Defined in: datagidx package.

Displays a glossary or index term with the first letter converted to uppercase. [§6.2]

\gls{[⟨*format*⟩]⟨*label*⟩}

Defined in: datagidx package.

Displays a glossary or index term. [§6.2]

\gls[⟨*options*⟩]{⟨*label*⟩}[⟨*insert*⟩]

Defined in: glossaries package.

Displays a glossary term according to its first use flag. [§6.1]

SUMMARY

\glsadd{⟨*label*⟩}

Defined in: datagidx package.

Adds the given entry to the glossary or index without displaying any text. [§6.2]

\glsadd[⟨*options*⟩]{⟨*label*⟩}

Defined in: glossaries package.

Adds the given entry to the glossary without displaying any text. [§6.1]

\glsaddall{⟨*database name*⟩}

Defined in: datagidx package.

Adds all the defined entries in the named database without displaying any text. [§6.2]

\glsaddall[⟨*options*⟩]

Defined in: glossaries package.

Adds all the defined entries without displaying any text. [§6.1]

\glsentryfirst{⟨*label*⟩}

Defined in: glossaries package.

Displays the value of the first key for a glossary entry. [§6.1]

\glsentrytext{⟨*label*⟩}

Defined in: glossaries package.

Displays the value of the text key for a glossary entry. [§6.1]

\Glspl[⟨*options*⟩]{⟨*label*⟩}[⟨*insert*⟩]

Defined in: glossaries package.

Displays the plural form of a glossary term according to its first use flag. The first letter of the plural text is converted to uppercase. [§6.1]

\Glspl{[⟨*format*⟩]⟨*label*⟩}

Defined in: datagidx package.

Displays the plural form of a glossary or index term with the first letter converted to uppercase. [§6.2]

\glspl{[⟨*format*⟩]⟨*label*⟩}

Defined in: datagidx package.

Displays the plural form of a glossary or index term. [§6.2]

\glspl[⟨*options*⟩]{⟨*label*⟩}[⟨*insert*⟩]

Defined in: glossaries package.

Displays the plural form of a glossary term according to its first use flag. [§6.1]

\glsreset{⟨*label*⟩}

Defined in: glossaries and datagidx packages.

Resets a glossary term's first use flag. [§6.1]

\glssymbol[⟨*options*⟩]{⟨*label*⟩}[⟨*insert*⟩]

Defined in: glossaries package.

Displays the symbol element of a glossary entry. [§6.1]

\glsunset{⟨*label*⟩}

Defined in: glossaries and datagidx packages.

Unsets a glossary term's first use flag. [§6.1]

\gram

Defined in: siunitx package.

Indicates a gram in commands like \si. [§4.9]

H

\headfont

Defined in: scrpage2 package.

Determines the font used by the header and footer with the scrplain and scrheadings page styles. [§4.2]

\headmark

Defined in: scrpage2 package.

Used in commands like \ihead to insert the current running header. [§4.2]

\hfill

Defined in: LaTeX Kernel.

Inserts a horizontal space that will expand to fit the available width. [§4.4]

\hspace{⟨*length*⟩}

Defined in: LaTeX Kernel.

Inserts a horizontal gap of the given width. [§4.4]

I

\If{⟨*condition*⟩}{⟨*block*⟩}

Defined in: algorithm2e package.

For use in algorithm-like environments to indicate an if-statement [§4.8]

\ifoot[⟨*scrplain*⟩]{⟨*scrheadings*⟩}

Defined in: scrpage2 package.

Indicates what to put in the inner footer area for the scrplain and scrheadings page styles. [§4.2]

\ihead[⟨*scrplain*⟩]{⟨*scrheadings*⟩}

Defined in: scrpage2 package.

Indicates what to put in the inner heading area for the scrplain and scrheadings page styles. [§4.2]

\include{⟨*file name*⟩}

Defined in: LaTeX Kernel.

Issues a \clearpage, creates an associated auxiliary file, inputs ⟨*file name*⟩ and issues another \clearpage. (See also \input.) [§3.0]

\includeonly⟨⟨*file list*⟩⟩

Defined in: LaTeX Kernel (Preamble Only).

Lists which of the files that are included using \include should be read in. Any files not in the list won't be included. [§3.0]

\index{⟨*text*⟩}

Defined in: LaTeX Kernel.

Adds indexing information to an external index file. The command \makeindex must be used in the preamble to enable this command. The external index file must be post-processed with an indexing application, such as makeindex. [§6.1]

\input{⟨*file name*⟩}

Defined in: LaTeX Kernel.

Reads in the contents of ⟨*file name*⟩. (See also \include.) [§3.0]

\itshape

Defined in: LaTeX Kernel.

Switches to the italic form of the current font family, if it exists. (See Volume 1 [15, §4.5.1].) [§4.2]

K

\kill

Defined in: tabbing environment.

Sets the tab stops defined in the line but won't typeset the actual line. [§4.6]

\kilo

Defined in: siunitx package.

Indicates a kilo multiplier in commands like \si. [§4.9]

\KwData{⟨*text*⟩}

Defined in: algorithm2e package.

For use in algorithm-like environments to indicate the algorithm input data [§4.8]

\KwIn{⟨*text*⟩}

Defined in: algorithm2e package.

For use in algorithm-like environments to indicate the algorithm input [§4.8]

\KwOut{⟨*text*⟩}

Defined in: algorithm2e package.

For use in algorithm-like environments to indicate the algorithm output [§4.8]

\KwResult{⟨*text*⟩}

Defined in: algorithm2e package.

For use in algorithm-like environments to indicate the algorithm output [§4.8]

\KwRet{⟨*value*⟩}

Defined in: algorithm2e package.

For use in algorithm-like environments to indicate a value returned [§4.8]

\KwTo

Defined in: algorithm2e package.

For use in algorithm-like environments to indicate "to" keyword [§4.8]

L

\label{⟨*string*⟩}

Defined in: LaTeX Kernel.

Assigns a unique textual label linked to the most recently incremented cross-referencing counter in the current scope. (See Volume 1 [15, §5.5].) [§2.0]

\large

Defined in: Most document classes.

Switches to large sized text. (See Volume 1 [15, §4.5.2].) [§4.1]

\leftarrow

Defined in: LaTeX Kernel (Math Mode).

Left arrow ←. (See Volume 1 [15, §9.4.7].) [§4.8]

\listoffigures

Defined in: Most classes that have the concept of document structure.

Inserts the list of figures. A second (possibly third) run is required to ensure the page numbering is correct. [§2.0]

\listoftables

Defined in: Most classes that have the concept of document structure.

Inserts the list of tables. A second (possibly third) run is required to ensure the page numbering is correct. [§2.0]

\lstinline[⟨*opts*⟩]⟨*char*⟩⟨*code*⟩⟨*char*⟩

Defined in: listings package.

Typesets ⟨*code*⟩ as an inline code snippet. [§4.5]

\lstinputlisting{⟨*options*⟩} {⟨*filename*⟩}

Defined in: listings package.

Reads in ⟨*filename*⟩ and typesets the contents as displayed code. [§4.5]

\begin{lstlisting}[⟨*options*⟩]

Defined in: listings package.

Typesets the contents of the environment as displayed code. [§4.5]

\lstlistoflistings

Defined in: listings package.

Prints a list of listings for those listings with the caption set. [§4.5]

\lstset{⟨*options*⟩}

Defined in: listings package.

Sets options used by the listings package. [§4.5]

\lvert

Defined in: amsmath (Math Mode).

Left vertical bar | delimiter. (See Volume 1 [15, §9.4.9].) [§4.8]

M

\mainmatter

Defined in: Most book-style classes, such as scrbook.

Switches to Arabic page numbering and enables chapter and section numbering. (See also \frontmatter and \backmatter.) [§2.0]

\makeglossaries

Defined in: glossaries package.

Activates \printglossaries (and \printglossary). [§6.1]

\makeindex

Defined in: LaTeX Kernel (Preamble Only).

Enables \index. [§6.1]

\MakeTextUppercase{⟨*text*⟩}

Defined in: textcase package.

Converts ⟨*text*⟩ to uppercase. [§6.2]

\maketitle

Defined in: Most classes that have the concept of a title page.

Generates the title page (or title block). This command is usually placed at the beginning of the document environment. [§2.0]

\MakeUppercase{⟨*text*⟩}

Defined in: LaTeX Kernel.

Converts its argument to upper case. [§5.1]

\mathbf{⟨*maths*⟩}

Defined in: LaTeX Kernel (Math Mode).

Renders ⟨*maths*⟩ in the predefined maths bold font. (Doesn't work with numbers and nonalphabetical symbols. See Volume 1 [15, §9.4.1].) [§4.8]

\mathcal{⟨*maths*⟩}

Defined in: LaTeX Kernel (Math Mode).

Typesets its argument in the maths calligraphic font. Example: $\mathcal{S}$ produces $\mathcal{S}$. (See Volume 1 [15, §9.4.1].) [§6.1]

\metre

Defined in: siunitx package.

Indicates the metre unit for use in commands like \si. [§4.9]

N

\newacro[⟨*options*⟩]{⟨*short*⟩}{⟨*long*⟩}

Defined in: datagidx package.

Defines a new acronym. [§6.2]

\newacronym[⟨*key-val list*⟩]{⟨*label*⟩}{⟨*abbrv*⟩}{⟨*long*⟩}

Defined in: glossaries package.

Shortcut that uses \newglossaryentry to define an acronym. [§6.1]

\newcommand{⟨*cmd*⟩}[⟨*n-args*⟩][⟨*default*⟩]{⟨*text*⟩}

Defined in: LaTeX Kernel.

Defines a new command. (See Volume 1 [15, §8].) [§4.2]

\newgidx{⟨*label*⟩}{⟨*title*⟩}

Defined in: datagidx package.

Defines a new index (or glossary) database. [§6.2]

`\newglossary[⟨log-ext⟩]{⟨name⟩}{⟨in-ext⟩}{⟨out-ext⟩}{⟨title⟩}[⟨counter⟩]`

Defined in: glossaries package.

Defines a new glossary. [§6.1]

`\newglossaryentry{⟨label⟩}{⟨key-val list⟩}`

Defined in: glossaries package.

Defines a new glossary entry or term. [§6.1]

`\newline`

Defined in: LATEX Kernel.

Forces a line break. [§4.7]

`\newterm[⟨options⟩]{⟨name⟩}`

Defined in: datagidx package.

Defines a new index or glossary term. [§6.2]

`\newtheorem{⟨name⟩}[⟨counter⟩] {⟨title⟩}[⟨outer counter⟩]`

Defined in: LATEX Kernel.

Defines a new theorem-like environment. The optional arguments are mutually exclusive. Some packages, such as ntheorem and amsthm, redefine this command to have a starred variant that defines unnumbered theorem-like environments. [§4.7]

`\newtheoremstyle{⟨name⟩}{⟨space above⟩}{⟨space below⟩}{⟨body font⟩}{⟨indent⟩}{⟨head font⟩}{⟨post head punctuation⟩}{⟨post head space⟩}{⟨head spec⟩}`

Defined in: amsthm package.

Defines a new theorem style called ⟨name⟩. [§4.7]

`\normalfont`

Defined in: LATEX Kernel.

Switches to the default font style. (See Volume 1 [15, §4.5.1].) [§4.2]

`\num{⟨number⟩}`

Defined in: siunitx package.

Typesets ⟨number⟩ with appropriate spacing. [§4.9]

O

`\ofoot[⟨scrplain⟩]{⟨scrheadings⟩}`

Defined in: scrpage2 package.

Indicates what to put in the outer footer area for the scrplain and scrheadings page styles. [§4.2]

`\ohead[⟨scrplain⟩]{⟨scrheadings⟩}`

Defined in: scrpage2 package.

Indicates what to put in the outer heading area for the scrplain and scrheadings page styles. [§4.2]

`\onehalfspacing`

Defined in: setspace package.

Switches to one-half line-spacing. [§4.3]

P

`\pagemark`

Defined in: scrpage2 package.

Used in commands like \ihead to insert the current page number. [§4.2]

`\pagenumbering{⟨style⟩}`

Defined in: LATEX Kernel.

Sets the style of the page numbers. [§2.0]

`\pagestyle{⟨style⟩}`

Defined in: LATEX Kernel.

Sets the style of the headers and footers. [§4.2]

`\par`

Defined in: LATEX Kernel.

Insert a paragraph break. [§1.0]

`\Parencite[⟨`*prenote*`⟩][⟨`*postnote*`⟩]`
`{⟨`*key*`⟩}`

Defined in: biblatex package.

Like `\parencite` but for use at the start of a sentence. [§5.3]

`\parencite[⟨`*prenote*`⟩][⟨`*postnote*`⟩]`
`{⟨`*key*`⟩}`

Defined in: biblatex package.

Like `\cite` but the citation is enclosed in parentheses. [§5.3]

`\parindent`

Defined in: LaTeX Kernel.

A length register that stores the indentation at the start of paragraphs. (See Volume 1 [15, §2.17].) [§4.7]

`\per`

Defined in: siunitx package.

Indicates a divider in commands like `\si`. [§4.9]

`\pnumfont`

Defined in: scrpage2 package.

Determines the font used by `\pagemark` with the scrplain and scrheadings page styles. [§4.2]

`\printbibliography[⟨`*options*`⟩]`

Defined in: biblatex package.

Prints the bibliography. [§5.3]

`\printglossaries`

Defined in: glossaries package.

Prints all of the defined glossaries. [§6.1]

`\printglossary[⟨`*key-val option list*`⟩]`

Defined in: glossaries package.

Prints the glossary identified in the optional argument or the default glossary if none identified. [§6.1]

`\printindex`

Defined in: makeidx package.

Prints the index. Must be used with `\makeindex` and `\index`. (The external index file must first be processed by an indexing application.) [§6.1]

`\PrintSemicolon`

Defined in: algorithm2e package.

Switches on the end of line semi-colon. (See also `\DontPrintSemicolon`.) [§4.8]

`\printterms[⟨`*options*`⟩]`

Defined in: datagidx package.

Displays the index or glossary or list of acronyms. [§6.2]

`\begin{Proof}[⟨`*title*`⟩]`

Defined in: ntheorem package with standard package option.

Typesets its contents as a proof. [§4.7]

`\begin{proof}[⟨`*title*`⟩]`

Defined in: amsthm package.

Typesets its contents as a proof. [§4.7]

`\publishers{⟨`*text*`⟩}`

Defined in: scrartcl, scrreprt, scrbook classes.

Specifies the publisher (set after all the other titling information). [§2.0]

Q

`\qedhere`

Defined in: amsthm package.

Overrides default location of QED marker in proof environment. [§4.7]

\qedsymbol

Defined in: amsthm package.

QED symbol used at the end of the proof environment. [§4.7]

R

\raggedright

Defined in: LaTeX Kernel.

Ragged-right paragraph justification. (See Volume 1 [15, §2.12].) [§4.1]

\raggedsection

Defined in: KOMA-Script classes, such as scrbook and scrreprt.

Governs the justification of headings. Defaults to \raggedright [§4.1]

\ref{⟨*string*⟩}

Defined in: LaTeX Kernel.

References the value of the counter linked to the given label. A second (possibly third) run of LaTeX is required to ensure the cross-references are up-to-date. (See Volume 1 [15, §5.5].) [§4.5]

\renewcommand{⟨*cmd*⟩}[⟨*n-args*⟩] [⟨*default*⟩]{⟨*text*⟩}

Defined in: LaTeX Kernel.

Redefines an existing command. (See Volume 1 [15, §8.2].) [§4.1]

\Return{⟨*value*⟩}

Defined in: algorithm2e package.

For use in algorithm-like environments to indicate a value returned [§4.8]

\rmfamily

Defined in: LaTeX Kernel.

Switches to the predefined serif font. (See Volume 1 [15, §4.5.1].) [§4.1]

\rvert

Defined in: amsmath (Math Mode).

Right vertical bar | delimiter. (See Volume 1 [15, §9.4.9].) [§4.8]

S

\scshape

Defined in: LaTeX Kernel.

Switches to the small-caps form of the current font family, if it exists. (See Volume 1 [15, §4.5.1].) [§4.7]

\second

Defined in: siunitx package.

Indicates the second unit for use in commands like \si. [§4.9]

\SI{⟨*number*⟩}{⟨*unit*⟩}

Defined in: siunitx package.

Typesets a number and unit, combining the functionality of \num and \si. [§4.9]

\si{⟨*unit*⟩}

Defined in: siunitx package.

Typesets the given unit. [§4.9]

\sim

Defined in: LaTeX Kernel (Math Mode).

Relational ~ symbol. [§4.7]

\singlespacing

Defined in: setspace package.

Switches to single line-spacing. [§4.3]

\sqrt[⟨*order*⟩]{⟨*operand*⟩}

Defined in: LaTeX Kernel (Math Mode).

Displays a root. (See Volume 1 [15, §9.4.6].) [§4.5]

\square⟨*unit*⟩

Defined in: siunitx package.

Indicates a squared unit in commands like \si. [§4.9]

\squared

Defined in: siunitx package.

Indicates a squared term in commands like \si after a unit command such as \metre. [§4.9]

\sum

Defined in: LaTeX Kernel (Math Mode).

Summation $\sum$ symbol. (See Volume 1 [15, §9.4.7].) [§4.8]

T

\begin{tabbing}

Defined in: LaTeX Kernel.

Allows you to define tab stops from the left margin. [§4.6]

\begin{table}[⟨*placement*⟩]

Defined in: Most classes that define sectioning commands.

Floats the contents to the nearest location according to the preferred placement options, if possible. Within the environment, \caption may be used one or more times, as required. (See Volume 1 [15, §7.2].) [§4.8]

\tableofcontents

Defined in: Most classes that have the concept of document structure.

Inserts the table of contents. A second (possibly third) run is required to ensure the page numbering is correct. [§2.0]

\textbf{⟨*text*⟩}

Defined in: LaTeX Kernel.

Renders ⟨*text*⟩ with a bold weight in the current font family, if it exists. (See Volume 1 [15, §4.5.1].) [§1.0]

\Textcite[⟨*prenote*⟩][⟨*postnote*⟩]{⟨*key*⟩}

Defined in: biblatex package.

Like \textcite but for use at the start of a sentence. [§5.3]

\textcite[⟨*prenote*⟩][⟨*postnote*⟩]{⟨*key*⟩}

Defined in: biblatex package.

Like \cite but designed for use in the flow of text. [§5.3]

\texttt{⟨*text*⟩}

Defined in: LaTeX Kernel.

Renders ⟨*text*⟩ in the predefined monospaced font. (See Volume 1 [15, §4.5.1].) [§6.1]

\begin{thebibliography}{⟨*widest entry label*⟩}

Defined in: Most classes that define sectioning commands.

Bibliographic list. (See Volume 1 [15, §5.6].) [§5.0]

\theorembodyfont{⟨*declarations*⟩}

Defined in: ntheorem package.

Changes the current theorem body fonts to ⟨*declarations*⟩. [§4.7]

\theoremheaderfont{⟨*declarations*⟩}

Defined in: ntheorem package.

Changes the current theorem header fonts to ⟨*declarations*⟩. [§4.7]

\theoremnumbering{⟨*style*⟩}

Defined in: ntheorem package.

Changes the current theorem numbering style to ⟨*style*⟩. [§4.7]

\theoremstyle{⟨*style name*⟩}

Defined in: ntheorem and amsthm packages.

\theoremstyle

Changes the current theorem style to ⟨*style name*⟩. [§4.7]

`\title{⟨text⟩}`

Defined in: Most classes that have the concept of a title page.

Specifies the document title. This command doesn't display any text so may be used in the preamble, but if it's not in the preamble it must be placed before `\maketitle`. [§2.0]

`\titlehead{⟨text⟩}`

Defined in: scrartcl, screprt, scrbook classes.

Specifies the title header (typeset at the top of the title page). [§2.0]

`\begin{titlepage}`

Defined in: Most classes that have the concept of a title page.

The contents of this environment are displayed on a single-column page with no header or footer and the page counter is set to 1. [§4.4]

`\ttfamily`

Defined in: LaTeX Kernel.

Switches to the predefined monospaced font. (See Volume 1 [15, §4.5.1].) [§4.5]

U

`\uElseIf{⟨condition⟩}{⟨block⟩}`

Defined in: algorithm2e package.

Like `\ElseIf` but doesn't put "end" after ⟨*block*⟩ [§4.8]

`\uIf{⟨condition⟩}{⟨block⟩}`

Defined in: algorithm2e package.

Like `\If` but doesn't put "end" after ⟨*block*⟩ [§4.8]

`\usepackage[⟨option-list⟩]{⟨package-list⟩}`

Defined in: LaTeX Kernel.

Loads the listed package(s). (See Volume 1 [15, §4.2].) [§2.0]

V

`\vec{⟨c⟩}`

Defined in: LaTeX Kernel (Math Mode).

Typesets its argument as a vector. (See Volume 1 [15, §9.4.11].) [§4.8]

`\vee`

Defined in: LaTeX Kernel (Math Mode).

Operator ∨ symbol. (See Volume 1 [15, §9.4.7].) [§4.7]

`\begin{verbatim}`

Defined in: LaTeX Kernel.

Typesets the contents of the environment as is. (Can't be used in the argument of a command.) [§4.5]

`\vfill`

Defined in: LaTeX Kernel.

Inserts a vertical space that will expand to fit the available height. [§4.4]

`\vspace{⟨length⟩}`

Defined in: LaTeX Kernel.

Inserts a vertical gap of the given height. [§4.4]

W

`\wedge`

Defined in: LaTeX Kernel (Math Mode).

Operator ∧ symbol. (See Volume 1 [15, §9.4.7].) [§4.7]

`\While{⟨condition⟩}{⟨body⟩}`

Defined in: algorithm2e package.

For use in algorithm-like environments to indicate a while-loop [§4.8]

`\title`

INDEX

Page numbers in **bold** indicate the entry definition in the summary.

tabbing environment

GNU Free Documentation License

Version 1.2, November 2002
Copyright © 2000,2001,2002 Free Software Foundation, Inc.

51 Franklin St, Fifth Floor, Boston, MA 02110-1301 USA

Preamble

The purpose of this License is to make a manual, textbook, or other functional and useful document "free" in the sense of freedom: to assure everyone the effective freedom to copy and redistribute it, with or without modifying it, either commercially or noncommercially. Secondarily, this License preserves for the author and publisher a way to get credit for their work, while not being considered responsible for modifications made by others.

This License is a kind of "copyleft", which means that derivative works of the document must themselves be free in the same sense. It complements the GNU General Public License, which is a copyleft license designed for free software.

We have designed this License in order to use it for manuals for free software, because free software needs free documentation: a free program should come with manuals providing the same freedoms that the software does. But this License is not limited to software manuals; it can be used for any textual work, regardless of subject matter or whether it is published as a printed book. We recommend this License principally for works whose purpose is instruction or reference.

1. APPLICABILITY AND DEFINITIONS

This License applies to any manual or other work, in any medium, that contains a notice placed by the copyright holder saying it can be distributed under the terms of this License. Such a notice grants a world-wide, royalty-free license, unlimited in duration, to use that work under the conditions stated herein. The "**Document**", below, refers to any such manual or work. Any member of the public is a licensee, and is addressed as "**you**". You accept the license if you copy, modify or distribute the work in a way requiring permission under copyright law.

A "**Modified Version**" of the Document means any work containing the Document or a portion of it, either copied verbatim, or with modifications and/or translated into another language.

A "**Secondary Section**" is a named appendix or a front-matter section of the Document that deals exclusively with the relationship of the publishers or authors of the Document to the Document's overall subject (or to related matters) and contains nothing that could fall directly within that overall subject. (Thus, if the Document is in part a textbook of mathematics, a Secondary Section may not explain any mathematics.) The relationship could be a matter of historical connection with the subject or with related matters, or of legal, commercial, philosophical, ethical or political position regarding them.

The **"Invariant Sections"** are certain Secondary Sections whose titles are designated, as being those of Invariant Sections, in the notice that says that the Document is released under this License. If a section does not fit the above definition of Secondary then it is not allowed to be designated as Invariant. The Document may contain zero Invariant Sections. If the Document does not identify any Invariant Sections then there are none.

The **"Cover Texts"** are certain short passages of text that are listed, as Front-Cover Texts or Back-Cover Texts, in the notice that says that the Document is released under this License. A Front-Cover Text may be at most 5 words, and a Back-Cover Text may be at most 25 words.

A **"Transparent"** copy of the Document means a machine-readable copy, represented in a format whose specification is available to the general public, that is suitable for revising the document straightforwardly with generic text editors or (for images composed of pixels) generic paint programs or (for drawings) some widely available drawing editor, and that is suitable for input to text formatters or for automatic translation to a variety of formats suitable for input to text formatters. A copy made in an otherwise Transparent file format whose markup, or absence of markup, has been arranged to thwart or discourage subsequent modification by readers is not Transparent. An image format is not Transparent if used for any substantial amount of text. A copy that is not "Transparent" is called **"Opaque"**.

Examples of suitable formats for Transparent copies include plain ASCII without markup, Texinfo input format, LaTeX input format, SGML or XML using a publicly available DTD, and standard-conforming simple HTML, PostScript or PDF designed for human modification. Examples of transparent image formats include PNG, XCF and JPG. Opaque formats include proprietary formats that can be read and edited only by proprietary word processors, SGML or XML for which the DTD and/or processing tools are not generally available, and the machine-generated HTML, PostScript or PDF produced by some word processors for output purposes only.

The **"Title Page"** means, for a printed book, the title page itself, plus such following pages as are needed to hold, legibly, the material this License requires to appear in the title page. For works in formats which do not have any title page as such, "Title Page" means the text near the most prominent appearance of the work's title, preceding the beginning of the body of the text.

A section **"Entitled XYZ"** means a named subunit of the Document whose title either is precisely XYZ or contains XYZ in parentheses following text that translates XYZ in another language. (Here XYZ stands for a specific section name mentioned below, such as **"Acknowledgements"**, **"Dedications"**, **"Endorsements"**, or **"History"**.) To **"Preserve the Title"** of such a section when you modify the Document means that it remains a section "Entitled XYZ" according to this definition.

The Document may include Warranty Disclaimers next to the notice which states that this License applies to the Document. These Warranty Disclaimers are considered to be included by reference in this License, but only as regards disclaiming warranties: any other implication that these Warranty Disclaimers may have is void and has no effect on the meaning of this License.

2. VERBATIM COPYING

You may copy and distribute the Document in any medium, either commercially or noncommercially, provided that this License, the copyright notices, and the license notice saying this License applies to the Document are reproduced in all copies, and that you add no other conditions whatsoever to those of this License. You may not use technical measures to obstruct or control the reading or further copying of the copies you make or distribute. However, you may accept compensation in exchange for copies. If you distribute a large enough number of copies you must also follow the conditions in section 3.

You may also lend copies, under the same conditions stated above, and you may publicly display copies.

3. COPYING IN QUANTITY

If you publish printed copies (or copies in media that commonly have printed covers) of the Document, numbering more than 100, and the Document's license notice requires Cover Texts, you must enclose the copies in covers that carry, clearly and legibly, all these Cover Texts: Front-Cover Texts on the front cover, and Back-Cover Texts on the back cover. Both covers must also clearly and legibly identify you as the publisher of these copies. The front cover must present the full title with all words of the title equally prominent and visible. You may add other material on the covers in addition. Copying with changes limited to the covers, as long as they preserve the title of the Document and satisfy these conditions, can be treated as verbatim copying in other respects.

If the required texts for either cover are too voluminous to fit legibly, you should put the first ones listed (as many as fit reasonably) on the actual cover, and continue the rest onto adjacent pages.

If you publish or distribute Opaque copies of the Document numbering more than 100, you must either include a machine-readable Transparent copy along with each Opaque copy, or state in or with each Opaque copy a computer-network location from which the general network-using public has access to download using public-standard network protocols a complete Transparent copy of the Document, free of added material. If you use the latter option, you must take reasonably prudent steps, when you begin distribution of Opaque copies in quantity, to ensure that this Transparent copy will remain thus accessible at the stated location until at least one year after the last time you distribute an Opaque copy (directly or through your agents or retailers) of that edition to the public.

It is requested, but not required, that you contact the authors of the Document well before redistributing any large number of copies, to give them a chance to provide you with an updated version of the Document.

4. MODIFICATIONS

You may copy and distribute a Modified Version of the Document under the conditions of sections 2 and 3 above, provided that you release the Modified Version under precisely this License, with the Modified Version filling the role of the Document, thus licensing distribution and modification of the Modified Version to whoever possesses a copy of it. In addition, you must do these things in the Modified Version:

A. Use in the Title Page (and on the covers, if any) a title distinct from that of the Document, and from those of previous versions (which should, if there were any, be listed in the History section of the Document). You may use the same title as a previous version if the original publisher of that version gives permission.

B. List on the Title Page, as authors, one or more persons or entities responsible for authorship of the modifications in the Modified Version, together with at least five of the principal authors of the Document (all of its principal authors, if it has fewer than five), unless they release you from this requirement.

C. State on the Title page the name of the publisher of the Modified Version, as the publisher.

D. Preserve all the copyright notices of the Document.

E. Add an appropriate copyright notice for your modifications adjacent to the other copyright notices.

F. Include, immediately after the copyright notices, a license notice giving the public permission to use the Modified Version under the terms of this License, in the form shown in the Addendum below.

G. Preserve in that license notice the full lists of Invariant Sections and required Cover Texts given in the Document's license notice.

H. Include an unaltered copy of this License.

I. Preserve the section Entitled "History", Preserve its Title, and add to it an item stating at least the title, year, new authors, and publisher of the Modified Version as given on the Title Page. If there is no section Entitled "History" in the Document, create one stating the title, year, authors, and publisher of the Document as given on its Title Page, then add an item describing the Modified Version as stated in the previous sentence.

J. Preserve the network location, if any, given in the Document for public access to a Transparent copy of the Document, and likewise the network locations given in the Document for previous versions it was based on. These may be placed in the "History" section. You may omit a network location for a work that was published at least four years before the Document itself, or if the original publisher of the version it refers to gives permission.

K. For any section Entitled "Acknowledgements" or "Dedications", Preserve the Title of the section, and preserve in the section all the substance and tone of each of the contributor acknowledgements and/or dedications given therein.

L. Preserve all the Invariant Sections of the Document, unaltered in their text and in their titles. Section numbers or the equivalent are not considered part of the section titles.

M. Delete any section Entitled "Endorsements". Such a section may not be included in the Modified Version.

N. Do not retitle any existing section to be Entitled "Endorsements" or to conflict in title with any Invariant Section.

O. Preserve any Warranty Disclaimers.

If the Modified Version includes new front-matter sections or appendices that qualify as Secondary Sections and contain no material copied from the Document, you may at your option designate some or all of these sections as invariant. To do this, add their titles to the list of Invariant Sections in the Modified Version's license notice. These titles must be distinct from any other section titles.

You may add a section Entitled "Endorsements", provided it contains nothing but endorsements of your Modified Version by various parties–for example, statements of peer review or that the text has been approved by an organization as the authoritative definition of a standard.

You may add a passage of up to five words as a Front-Cover Text, and a passage of up to 25 words as a Back-Cover Text, to the end of the list of Cover Texts in the Modified Version. Only one passage of Front-Cover Text and one of Back-Cover Text may be added by (or through arrangements made by) any one entity. If the Document already includes a cover text for the same cover, previously added by you or by arrangement made by the same entity you are acting on behalf of, you may not add another; but you may replace the old one, on explicit permission from the previous publisher that added the old one.

The author(s) and publisher(s) of the Document do not by this License give permission to use their names for publicity for or to assert or imply endorsement of any Modified Version.

5. COMBINING DOCUMENTS

You may combine the Document with other documents released under this License, under the terms defined in section 4 above for modified versions, provided that you include in the combination all of the Invariant Sections of all of the original documents, unmodified, and list them all as Invariant Sections of your combined work in its license notice, and that you preserve all their Warranty Disclaimers.

The combined work need only contain one copy of this License, and multiple identical Invariant Sections may be replaced with a single copy. If there are multiple Invariant Sections with the same name but different contents, make the title of each such section unique by adding at the end of it, in parentheses, the name of the original author or publisher of that section if known, or else a unique number. Make the same adjustment to the section titles in the list of Invariant Sections in the license notice of the combined work.

In the combination, you must combine any sections Entitled "History" in the various original documents, forming one section Entitled "History"; likewise combine any sections Entitled "Acknowledgements", and any sections Entitled "Dedications". You must delete all sections Entitled "Endorsements".

6. COLLECTIONS OF DOCUMENTS

You may make a collection consisting of the Document and other documents released under this License, and replace the individual copies of this License in the various documents with a single copy that is included in the collection, provided that you follow the rules of this License for verbatim copying of each of the documents in all other respects.

You may extract a single document from such a collection, and distribute it individually under this License, provided you insert a copy of this License into the extracted document, and follow this License in all other respects regarding verbatim copying of that document.

7. AGGREGATION WITH INDEPENDENT WORKS

A compilation of the Document or its derivatives with other separate and independent documents or works, in or on a volume of a storage or distribution medium, is called an "aggregate" if the copyright resulting from the compilation is not used to limit the legal rights of the compilation's users beyond what the individual works permit. When the Document is included in an aggregate, this License does not apply to the other works in the aggregate which are not themselves derivative works of the Document.

If the Cover Text requirement of section 3 is applicable to these copies of the Document, then if the Document is less than one half of the entire aggregate, the Document's Cover Texts may be placed on covers that bracket the Document within the aggregate, or the electronic equivalent of covers if the Document is in electronic form. Otherwise they must appear on printed covers that bracket the whole aggregate.

8. TRANSLATION

Translation is considered a kind of modification, so you may distribute translations of the Document under the terms of section 4. Replacing Invariant Sections with translations requires special permission from their copyright holders, but you may include translations of some or all Invariant Sections in addition to the original versions of these Invariant Sections. You may include a translation of this License, and all the license notices in the Document, and any Warranty Disclaimers, provided that you also include the original English version of this License and the original versions of those notices and disclaimers. In case of a disagreement between the translation and the original version of this License or a notice or disclaimer, the original version will prevail.

If a section in the Document is Entitled "Acknowledgements", "Dedications", or "History", the requirement (section 4) to Preserve its Title (section 1) will typically require changing the actual title.

9. TERMINATION

You may not copy, modify, sublicense, or distribute the Document except as expressly provided for under this License. Any other attempt to copy, modify, sublicense or distribute the Document is void, and will automatically terminate your rights under this License. However, parties who have received copies, or rights, from you under this License will not have their licenses terminated so long as such parties remain in full compliance.

10. FUTURE REVISIONS OF THIS LICENSE

The Free Software Foundation may publish new, revised versions of the GNU Free Documentation License from time to time. Such new versions will be similar in spirit to the present version, but may differ in detail to address new problems or concerns. See http://www.gnu.org/copyleft/.

Each version of the License is given a distinguishing version number. If the Document specifies that a particular numbered version of this License "or any later version" applies to it, you have the option of following the terms and conditions either of that specified version or of any later version that has been published (not as a draft) by the Free Software Foundation. If the Document does not specify a version number of this License, you may choose any version ever published (not as a draft) by the Free Software Foundation.

ADDENDUM: How to use this License for your documents

To use this License in a document you have written, include a copy of the License in the document and put the following copyright and license notices just after the title page:

Copyright © YEAR YOUR NAME. Permission is granted to copy, distribute and/or modify this document under the terms of the GNU Free Documentation License, Version 1.2 or any later version published by the Free Software Foundation; with no Invariant Sections, no Front-Cover Texts, and no Back-Cover Texts. A copy of the license is included in the section entitled "GNU Free Documentation License".

If you have Invariant Sections, Front-Cover Texts and Back-Cover Texts, replace the "with ... Texts." line with this:

> with the Invariant Sections being LIST THEIR TITLES, with the Front-Cover Texts being LIST, and with the Back-Cover Texts being LIST.

If you have Invariant Sections without Cover Texts, or some other combination of the three, merge those two alternatives to suit the situation.

If your document contains nontrivial examples of program code, we recommend releasing these examples in parallel under your choice of free software license, such as the GNU General Public License, to permit their use in free software.

HISTORY

16th March, 2013 (Version 1.3)

- Added recap on building the document.

- Added sections on `latexmk` and `arara`.

- Changed examples to use KOMA.

- Added sections on `jabref`, natbib and biblatex.

- Added information about the listings, siunitx, amsthm, ntheorem and algorithm2e packages.

- Added section on datagidx to the chapter on indexes and glossaries.

- Added summary section.

- Some sections have been reordered.

- Removed section on modifying textual tags such as \contentsname (now in Volume 1).

Back Cover Text

Lightning Source UK Ltd.
Milton Keynes UK
UKHW031818160421
382119UK00008B/1457